*DFS
T
L
C*

Laura

MISFIT

CHAMPIONS

Sustainable Business Basics

Setting Up Effective HR in Your Small Business or Startup

By Art Espey & Laura Bowser

OWL PUBLISHING

Owl Publishing, LLC.
www.owlpublishinghouse.com

717-925-7511

ISBN:

Library of Congress Control Number: In Process

DEDICATION

"Coming together is a beginning, staying together is progress, and working together is success."

— Henry Ford

This book is dedicated to our families who have weathered the joys and pains of our entrepreneurial experiences over the years.

Espey & Bowser

CONTENTS

PREFACE

After years of both of us working with start-ups, small businesses, and multiple accelerator and incubator programs, we noticed something. Startups and incubator programs often entirely ignore Human Resources and they are doing themselves no favors.

As experienced leaders in startups, middle market companies and small businesses, we get it. For the average small company or start-up, HR probably isn't top of mind. Creating and building a product and scaling your company's top-line growth consumes most of your day-to-day activities. But what about your people strategy? How will you grow without having one?

As mentors in the small business and start-up space, we have noticed a dangerous pattern. HR isn't just a non-priority; it is often being neglected entirely. We have seen far too many small business owners consider HR a backburner task, placed permanently in the parking lot of their business strategy; or they do the bare minimum for compliance purposes only. But what happens when it blows up in the business owner's face? The reality is that it is not an "if", but a "when". People leadership is a messy business. And if neglected, it can shut a small business or start-up down.

Don't believe us? Let's look at the statistics. SHRM is an organization dedicated to the elevation and impact of Human Resources. SHRM states that 54 percent of small businesses handle employment matters themselves, often to save money, but this also means that the CEOs and founders can neglect their HR responsibilities in favor of sales, technology, and other critical business functions. When business owners handle their employment matters without the support of a HR professional, their sales, technology, and growth suffer since they must divide their focus. They have little to no real understanding of HR outside of previous work experience or input from financial and benefit advisors. As a result, their Talent and HR strategies are piecemeal at best.

Without efficient human resource practices, the lack of strategy focused on employee performance, retention, and loyalty, will only lead to your business struggling to achieve its goals and objectives. Still not convinced? There are dozens of statistics to back up how important HR for small businesses really is. According to ConnectTeam.com here are just a few:

- Businesses invested in a strong candidate experience will increase their hire quality by 70%.

- Almost 80% of workers say that they prefer new or additional benefits over a pay increase.

- 75% of employees will stay longer at a company that proactively listens to and addresses their issues and concerns.

- Disengaged employees are nearly twice as likely as engaged employees to look for new jobs.

- 71% of Millennials are more likely to leave their employer because they're unhappy with how their leadership skills are being developed.

- 79% of workers said that company culture is an important job satisfaction factor.

- Just 25% of employees who quit their jobs said that money was the main reason they chose to leave.

- Employees said that if their company provides equal opportunities, they're about four times more likely to be proud to work for that company.

While these are just a few statistics, dozens more can be found at SHRM.org and various business publications online. The reality is that your company will fail if people and policy management is not a key part of your overall business strategy.

The following book reflects some general guidance and leading principles based on our experience regarding HR while leading growth in businesses. Our goal is to condense the areas of most importance to small businesses and startups, and to take away some of the fear and misunderstanding that small business owners and entrepreneurs have when it comes to HR.

You know the old expression that knowledge is power? We aren't making you an expert, but we are arming you with the information you need as a leader in order to tackle some of the most common HR challenges.

Welcome to your crash course!

Laura and Art

INTRODUCTION

Most people have dreamt of owning their own business at some point in their lives. They find something that they are good at, or really enjoy doing, and decide to share it with others.

They read books, they watch YouTube videos, they talk to people, they make a plan and over time they accomplish goals that they never thought they'd be able to achieve. They are doing something that they love. Then, as their business starts to pick up, they realize that they need help. They hire one person, then two. The next thing they know, they have a few people working for them with nothing but shoddy rules and policies to consistently lead by.

At this stage one of two things happens:

1. They realize they have to define the people policies and processes, make sure they comply with all the appropriate governmental laws, rules and regulations and then effectively communicate them back to all team members.

OR

2. As in many cases, they have a people problem that festers and escalates and becomes a multi-year legal issue.

Oh, and saying, "well, that will never happen to me," significantly increases the odds that it will. And that is why we wrote this book.

It is for the small business owner or entrepreneur who wants to make sure that both their team members and the business have a fun, value laden, long-term, mutually beneficial relationship. Happy team members produce more and help businesses grow. People are happier when the rules and expectations are clear and consistent and they are given the space to perform and grow.

As we'll discuss later, almost 25% of the small businesses that fail go down in flames because of people issues. Maybe HR is important.

We hope you find value in this HR primer. If you have an HR team that handles all of this, then this may be too basic for you.

If you don't, keep reading!

1

HR in Start-ups and Small Businesses

Oftentimes when the word HR gets thrown around, thoughts of compliance training or an employee poster campaign comes to mind. Maybe this is because the term "Human Resources" in itself doesn't sound as tangible as something like Risk, Procurement, or Finance; or maybe this is because of a personal interaction with a previous employer's HR department. Whatever it is, that image is a dangerous illusion and needs to be erased from your mind.

HR is messy and never for the faint of heart. Employees are all too human, and their work and private lives unfortunately overlap. Unlike a computer that IT can fix, you can't restart a human, or put them in rice to dry out. There are no hacks. Each employee is different and has unique needs. Add to this the endlessly evolving federal and state labor laws, along with your organization's interpersonal dynamics, and now suddenly the idea of HR is overwhelming.

Many small businesses and startups have experienced significant people challenges over the last few years. Remote work mandates due to the COVID-19 pandemic and the management of political and social dialogue in the workplace are just two of the recent people issues that can challenge a business.

The fact that most businesses fail within their first five years is hardly news to any entrepreneur or business owner. This statistic gets thrown around so much it almost feels like it is predestined for some start-ups, or some kind of sales technique by accelerators to get you to sign-up to their next great start-up program. Now, we are not suggesting that incubators, accelerators, and/or mentor programs are not of great value. They are. But they almost always focus on investing, pitching, branding, financial management, and legal. HR often remains removed from the picture entirely, which sadly reinforces the normalcy that founders should choose to ignore HR basics until they reach a certain size. This is true for small businesses as well.

Cash flow is, as it should be, your primary focus. HR usually takes a backseat to other business needs. And this can happen fast and out of nowhere.

On the rare occasion that a small business has some HR processes, it oftentimes is because the founder dumped the task on their administrative support (i.e. The Bookkeeper or Administrative Assistant). This is not surprising since founders are normally subject matter experts and bring little HR savvy to their company. That said, it is dangerous. While in the following chapters we explore the various reasons why, the most basic reason is because the Bookkeeper or Administrative Assistant is not an expert at navigating conflict. And let's face it, the first or second hire a founder makes is never an HR manager. This is for a good reason. That said, throw in a few more hires and suddenly there is a small team of 4-12 people who lack a designated employee who understands HR and who can assist when issues arise…and they will arise.

Every small business owner or start-up founder feels like they are up against the clock. Product features must be tested, and cash flow is always top of mind. If you are the founder of a start-up who is managing a capital raise you are also dealing with investor meetings, pitch competitions, and marketing research. This endless, yet not wholly inclusive list, results in most small businesses taking massive shortcuts on operational needs.

A few years back, Entrepreneur.com did a survey and shared an infographic with all the reasons that start-ups and small businesses fail. Not surprisingly the main reason was a lack of cash or investor interest. But coming in a very close second, it was found that 23% of startups fail because they don't have the right people working on their team.

Interestingly, there's a reason why accelerators, or buyers of small businesses, prefer teams with a history of working together. When investors ask for resumes and for a team overview slide, they aren't just checking the team's credentials, they want to understand each and every key player. What are the interpersonal dynamics? What are the retention rates? What are the legal and operating agreements between all parties? Why? Because if one key person decides they don't want to build anymore and quits, the game can be over. The company can fail. And this is heartbreaking because while no one can ensure your business will be successful, or that you will land a huge investor, an HR plan for your business can solve this problem. Likewise, if the above-mentioned survey is correct, **a solid HR plan can reduce the chance of your small business collapsing by one-fourth. That is 25%.**

Do we have your attention now? Good! Let's dive in.

2

HR is Your Ally

HR is a tool to use to develop a sustainable business. As you grow your company, HR becomes a thought process not just a department. Think of HR as IT. In the 1980s when technology really started to change the way business operated, IT was relegated to the basement of all large companies—completely siloed. Functionally, it was used only when a machine broke, and few departments had any type of IT plan. Fast forward 40 years and IT is now integrated into every department and company in the world. It's the heart of everything in modern day business. HR should be treated the same because it is not a standalone department. It is how you scale and grow your business. It is how you compete for talent. It is at the heart of your culture and strategy.

As a small business leader, your HR consultant should become an invaluable sounding board. If they aren't, you are not working with the right person. It is imperative that you get to know them and their strengths. Likewise, their role is to understand your management style and your blindspots. Trust becomes imperative in the relationship, and it is not uncommon that HR becomes one of the first calls you make when discussing an impending business decision. This includes, a variety of management matters, such as but not limited to:

- A sounding board on delicate personnel issues where the answer isn't immediately clear. We have already mentioned how messy human relations is. You can read all the HR books in the world but at the end of the day it is not uncommon that the answer is never completely cut and dry.

- For training, development, hiring advice—or support on giving constructive feedback to employees.

- For advice on risk management. Oftentimes this means protecting the company, and yourself, during a touchy personnel issue, a termination process or legal matter.

As we mentioned above, trust is imperative. Find the support that best suits your company's needs and growth strategy. Your HR go-to person is key to providing your company with the intellectual capacity to grow.

Think of it this way, sales is the air that keeps your business going. Just like starving your body of the air you breathe leads to an untimely demise, starving your company of sales does the same to it. Without sales, no business can survive long-term. HR is like the blood that flows through your body making sure every part has what it needs to operate at its best and carrying away what is not needed for the good of the whole. The people on your team are needed to operate at their best so that the company can continue to move forward.

Your people policies will ultimately drive your customer policies. This determines the culture of the organization that you lead. You can have a great vision and mission, but if the people policies don't support it then it is little more than a dream or a wish.

Your people policies are based on your values—but are not just what you say your values are—that, quite frankly, is little more than talk. Actions, in this case, truly speak louder than words.

Your first few hires will determine the tone and pace of your company culture. Some of it will be great and some of it you will want to alter slightly as you add more team members. You will, at first, be uncomfortable with relinquishing control over certain aspects of the business. You should be very reluctant about giving up involvement in any aspect of the people issues that may arise in your business.

Company culture means different things to different people but sum it up as the way that your team operates and collaborates to solve your customers' problems and grow the business. Do they cut corners and accept small mistakes to get things done fast, or do they take the appropriate amount of time to make sure things are done right the first time? Do they continuously bad mouth customers with a level of disdain, that though shared jokingly amongst themselves, could leak out at a critical time? Culture is about the tenor and tone that you as the leader set for the team members to march by. Your first few hires, by their actions, both intentional and unintentional, have the power to alter the culture without you even knowing it. The same goes for your HR consultant. To learn more about building a great culture please read our previous book in the Misfit Champion's

Sustainable Business Series—Building A Culture of Accountability.

Having a clear understanding of what you need to be successful shows strength and keeps you grounded. Communicating these needs with your team helps keep you accountable and well supported.

3

HR TECHNICAL COMPETENCIES FOR DUMMIES

We know you are not dumb, but Human Resources is probably one of the more complicated aspects of running a small business. The complexities of working and dealing with people's emotions and developmental needs can't be solved on a spreadsheet or through a PowerPoint presentation. Yet, HR is incredibly important. It has become even more relevant, as seen recently during the COVID-19 crisis, when many companies have had to take on the additional burden of supporting remote work and supporting employees' health and wellness as they navigate a new lifestyle. Employee salaries and benefits usually make up a huge chunk of business operating expenses. This is especially true if you run a consulting firm or are in a service-based industry.

In order to fully grasp the function HR plays in your small business, you need to understand what Human Resource Management (HRM) is, and what it is not. Simply put, Human Resources (HR) is the department, or person, within your business that is responsible for all things employee related. That includes recruiting, vetting, selecting, hiring, onboarding, training, promoting, paying, relocating, and firing employees and independent contractors. HR is also the department that stays on top of new legislation guiding how workers need to be treated during their full employee lifecycle – from recruitment to leaving the organization. This includes legal rights, safety, benefits, protected categories, leave policies, and more.

According to the Society for Human Resource Management (SHRM) there are 15 HR functional areas of expertise within HR. Now, you are likely thinking I don't need to understand all 15, and to some extent that is true, but you do need to understand how complicated HR is in order to find the right HR resources for your organization. While it is true that in order to be HR certified, one must understand each functional HR area, let us be very clear—when a person has the title HR specialist, the first question you need to ask is "a specialist in which functional area?"

Sadly, many executives and founders, even in fortune 500 companies, assume that all HR practitioners do the same job. This couldn't be further from the truth. In reality, HR has many areas of expertise. One HR practitioners' sole purpose could be compliance, another organizational development, another labor relations, etc. Just like all doctors are not the same, HR practitioners are not either. You wouldn't go to your dermatologist to have brain surgery. Don't make that same mistake by hiring the wrong HR advisor. HR can be very complicated. Let us give you an example. The Health Care Reform law that passed in 2010 was over 2,000 pages long. How many small business leaders do you know who read it? And of the many laws passed that year, that was just one law of thousands which included dozens of changes that impacted small businesses. If you aren't proactively seeking council or

HR advice on labor laws, bad things can happen to your company—ranging from legal or regulatory penalties to having to shut down. So make sure you hire the correct HR practitioner for your organizational needs. In this case an HR advisor specializing in legal compliance, or an attorney, would be who you would want to seek guidance from.

In addition to HR Specialist, there are other HR titles that business owners seeking advice should be aware of when reviewing resumes for possible HR hires or consulting services. These include HR Leader, HR Manager, Generalists, and HR Business Partner.

HR Managers are exactly how it sounds. These are managers of units within a specific HR function for an organization. Oftentimes, this is a person who manages a group of HR specialists. HR Generalists (also known as HR Practitioners) are individuals who are familiar with all HR functions. While they might be a specialist in one or two areas of HR, they know enough about all HR functions to give advice on how to move forward. This role/title is exactly what a small business owner should be looking for when searching for a HR advisor, or person to lead their small business's HR department. While a Generalist might not always have the answers, they know enough to know what they don't know and where to find what is needed. That is key when it comes to getting HR right within your organization.

The other titles of HR Leaders and/or HR Business Partners are usually just high-ranking HR Generalists within large corporations who have general experience in most fields of HR, and who play a very strategic role within their organization. While highly experienced, it is rare that a small business would need to make a hire of this level of expertise unless your business is scaling at an unprecedented rate.

As previously mentioned, HR contains fifteen functional areas. All fifteen areas can be subdivided into three technical competencies: People, Organization, and Workplace. This is useful to understand because oftentimes an HR Generalist will be most versed in one area of technical competency. Knowing which area your organization needs support in the most can assist you in finding the right hire or fractional advisor. The following chart lists each Technical Competency with the corresponding functional areas underneath.

While overwhelming to think about as a business owner, for small businesses the most important functional areas include all areas under People, and the US Employment Law & Regulation area under Workforce. While the rest of the functional areas are important, they often are more focused on medium sized to large businesses and sometimes inapplicable to organizations of under 100 employees.

Knowledge Domains

3 Domains
————
15 Functional Areas

People

HR Strategic Planning
Talent Acquisition
Employee Engagement & Retention
Learning & Development
Total Rewards

Organization

Structures of the HR Function
Organizational Effectiveness & Development
Workforce Management
Employee & Labor Relations
Technology management

Workplace

HR in the Global Context
Diversity & Inclusion
Risk Management
Corporate Social Responsibility
Employment Law & Regulations

In the following chapters we will walk you through several best practices and experiences. Most are focused on various aspects of the People domain. We will also discuss US Employment laws and regulation basics.

Your employees are one of your greatest assets. You must protect and lead that asset. A company is defined by the people who work there. Without the right people, a company won't have growth, performance, or stability. Without those three things, a company will not succeed.

4

You've Hired HR Support. Now What?

The process each small business takes when creating a human resource department may differ. A brand new organization will follow a different path than one that has been in operation for some time and has made the decision to add or hire outside HR assistance.

It is also important to know that the role of HR within your business is affected by the current size of the organization. For example, if you have over 15 employees, your organization must comply with Title VII of the Civil Rights Act which instructs you to make sure you don't discriminate against protected categories. And if you have over 50 employees, your organization is responsible for FMLA (Family Medical Leave Act) (Note: If you have over 50 employees and no HR support you are likely in violation of several labor laws at this point).

Additionally, the amount of support and infrastructure already in place, and the industry you are in, also plays into how you will approach developing your HR policies and procedures. If you are a start-up, there will likely be very little review as few policies and procedures will have yet to have been put into place. However, if you have been in business for several years and are just now bringing in HR support, a full HR audit of current policies, procedures and assets will be required before HR planning can move forward.

Conducting a full HR Audit

The first step in forming an HR department in an existing organization is a full assessment of the current state of all HR-related activities. This is normally in the form of an audit. While audits can be scary, for a smaller company, the time and cost of conducting audits is not usually for improving HR efficiencies, but rather proactive defense against the expense of possible future litigation and/or fines and penalties by the Department of Labor.

There are many different types of HR audits. An audit can be as simple as reviewing employment files to ensure that they are in order, or it can involve reviewing effectiveness of policies, which may require collecting qualitative data through focus groups and interviews. Audits can be broad or very tailored. But when building an HR department from the ground up, you as a business owner will want to launch a full Compliance Audit to start.

A Compliance Audit focuses on how well the organization is complying with current federal, state, and local laws and regulations. This will require the review of all employee and 1099 files and labor designations, hiring and off-boarding policies and procedures, payroll and taxes, and all legal documents and agreements. It is not uncommon for your HR consultant or hire to need the support of a employment lawyer in this process. The output from a Compliance Audit will include strengths and immediate steps required to bring your business into full legal compliance, as well as a list of missing documents and/or policies that must be corrected.

> *"While never fun, do not drag your feet on conducting this! It could save your small business. Many years ago a local non-profit I was volunteering with went through a compliance audit. This particular organization was over a decade in age and had unfortunately waited too long to establish HR support. During the audit, it was discovered that several employees had actually been misclassified as 1099 contractors. By misclassifying over 5 years of employees, the organization wasn't paying unemployment and other taxes when it should have been. The result was the organization had to repay all of those taxes and benefits that they hadn't been paying to well over 5 employees. This miscalculation almost bankrupted the non-profit and it took months for them to get out of the red."*
> *-Laura*

Running a Compliance Audit is important because it not only helps your business mitigate risks, and possible penalties, it also helps establish new best practices for onboarding and exiting your employees and contractors. It shines a bright light on a vulnerable blind spot.

It is important to understand that a Compliance Audit is time consuming, and the length of time required is determined by the age of your small business. Don't get impatient. This step is vitally important because best practices and strategic planning are both impacted by the results of this audit. Once your organization is fully compliant, you can begin to build your HR plan.

Building HR from the Ground Up

HR professionals serve many roles within an organization. Once an organization is fully compliant, the next steps will depend on the results of your audit and your goals as a business owner. It may be that you are expecting a huge growth phase, or it may be that you run a small family business and the founder is about to retire. Wherever your small business is on its journey determines the immediate focus for your HR team.

For example, if you are now entering into a high-growth phase, establishing a staffing plan, and determining your organization's recruiting practices, becomes the number one priority. However, if you are a small family owned business about to transition leadership, culture change and communications might become the focus. You as the small business owner must work with your HR support team to determine what to prioritize next based on your organizational strategy. There is not a clear or correct path as to what to build out first. That said, there are certain plans and requirements that must be fulfilled based on your organizational priorities. Those include:

- The creation of an HR staffing plan
- An HR budget
- Job descriptions
- Pay structure and compensation analysis
- Benefits plans
- Employee handbook
- Safety procedures
- Employment posters and labor laws
- Hiring procedures and firing procedures
- Personnel files and asset management
- Performance evaluation processes

While we will briefly cover many of the topics listed above in this book, your job as a business owner is not to delve that far into the weeds. That is the job of your HR consultant and/or team. The amount of work required by your HR team will be proportional to the size and the development of your company.

Your job as a founder or business leader is to steer the ship. Define your company values, the principles on which you want to build, and hire the right HR resources to help you achieve that. Remember when we said trust is key in who you bring in to help establish your HR processes? This is why. It is not your job to manage every detail of your company's human capital processes. It's your job to hire the right person who can, and the rest will follow.

Communicating intent is key in developing of team members because through that communication, leaders establish and build trust. Once you have established a foundation of trust, the team can really start to grow and do some incredible things. The goal is to create an environment that both empowers and enriches team members and customers, and quite frankly, if done correctly, all stakeholders.

5

DON'T HIRE FAST.
DON'T FIRE SLOW.

The expression, "Hire slow, and fire fast" gets thrown around a lot. Some would even argue it has become a cliché as it oversimplifies the hiring and firing process. In recent years the expression has been wordsmithed into "Hire fast, fire faster," but that isn't quite the point. The core message behind the expression challenges a sad truth—most start-ups and small businesses hire fast and fire slow.

As a business owner you must be deliberate about your hiring and firing strategies. Moving too fast to fill a role likely means you failed to perform due diligence and/or hire the right talent.

In a small business you cannot afford to have one person on staff that is subpar, or worse, a bad apple. And yet, oftentimes the same small business owner, once they recognize they made a bad hiring decision, fails to act. Realizing they moved too fast, they slow down. As the leader of your company, it is your responsibility to act fast. According to the U.S. Department of Labor, a bad hire can cost you up to 30 percent of that employee's salary—and that assumes that once fired they don't legally challenge you.

> *Years ago, I was doing some work with a high-growth small business and I witnessed first-hand what happens when an underperforming employee is not let go. Sadly, in this case, the employee was also sabotaging others' careers. For months, the business owner chose to try and work with the employee—actually gave* the *employee more power and responsibility. The thought was perhaps the new role would motivate the employee and build loyalty. This couldn't have been further from the truth. The result was massive turnover, and the eventual discovery of*

> *unethical behavior on the part of the employee*
> *which would later cost the company hundreds of*
> *thousands of dollars.*

> *-Laura*

It is never compassionate to keep a bad employee as it crushes the morale of the entire team. What this business owner painfully learned was that one person, just one, has the ability to destroy a small business; and can make the entire team struggle as a result. The owner failed to realize that the right thing for their business was to let this employee go.

So how does a small business avoid making a bad hire? In the previously mentioned example, the outcome could have been avoided had tougher choices been made and had a more structured hiring and firing process been in place. While an HR consultant or HR manager can develop a hiring process for your organization, it is important as a business owner to hold yourself accountable. Accountability often looks like asking yourself a series of questions and then answering those questions very truthfully.

Do you hire out of fear or pressure?

To start, do not hire fast out of fear for a deliverable. While this seems easy enough, we have rarely seen small businesses not make this mistake. For example, it often starts with a large RFP, item order, or grant. Your team works hard to close the deal. Then the call comes, and you learn that you just landed the $800k deal and now have a 5-month turnaround time. But your team is already at capacity. In fact, everyone was too busy to pull together the job descriptions and start the search on a project that wasn't a done deal. Now, you as the CEO, have to hire fast in order to meet deadlines. There isn't time to fully vet candidates through multiple rounds of interviews. Worse, make the wrong hire and the reputation of your organization is on the line.

This nightmare situation happens frequently and yet can easily be avoided if you bring in HR support early on in the business development process. Likewise, this situation can also be avoided if you, as a leader, are proactively building your company's talent pipeline.

Do You "Future Truth" Your Pipeline?

If you aren't, start. The idea of "future truthing" is quite simple. Make a statement that will be true and hold yourself accountable to it. This is not meant to be a public statement. This is for you personally as a small business owner. Future truthing is similar to strategic planning on the fly. It's the concept of aligning your future vision with short-term goals for getting there.

As a business owner you might only have 5 employees, but if your goal is $15M in revenue in two years, then your future truth may be 40+ hires in under 2 years. That future truth requires a constant pipeline of talent regardless of whether you have the cash flow to make a single hire just yet. And remember the nightmare situation mentioned above? A pipeline of talent is a quick solve when managing large deliverables and projects.

Future truthing helps you avoid the trap of hiring based on waves of need. Instead, ***have candidates in mind before a position opens***. And in some cases, if you see a talent that blows you away, consider finding a way to hire that person now. One of the key things to remember is you should never be scrambling to fill a position. You should already have a pipeline of potential candidates that you can access who you know are pre-qualified.

Now, we know you are thinking that this could be a full-time job. And, to some extent, it is fair to say this requires a lot of time and planning. However, as the leader of your company you should be playing a key role within your culture. Creating a culture of recruiting is one way to do that. Work to deliberately build the team you want as a business leader. Don't be afraid to say, "I can't hire you now but when we hit X in revenue goals, I would love to bring you in and make you a part of the team."

Once you build a pipeline, make sure you nurture it. Communicate with potential candidates frequently—even over the course of months to years. Invite them to your company events. Get to know them. Celebrate their successes online. If possible, build loyalty and trust even before making an offer. It will make the onboarding process of that employee so much easier.

Are you as the founder the face of your company's recruitment efforts?

Oftentimes business owners mistakenly dump all recruitment upon their HR support. This is a HUGE mistake. Why? Because your company culture should be deliberately created through **YOUR** recruitment process. Recruitment is not interviewing. It is not posting a job description either. Recruiting is selling which is rarely a strength within HR.

When you meet with a potential candidate, or network with others at events, you are showcasing what your company has to offer with a focus on the culture you as the leader are working to build. Done correctly you will begin to establish a target audience and a pipeline of interest. But you alone should not be the only person selling. Let your employees sell as well. Their referrals could bring outstanding candidates in, which in turn, helps them feel more buy-in to their role. Afterall, every employee plays a role in building your company's culture, particularly when it's small.

Are you building a feedback culture?

As soon as you onboard a new employee, begin building and normalizing a feedback and coaching culture with them. There are many advantages to training your team on how to give and receive feedback effectively. This is especially important for any of your people managers. And while we will not tell you what can and will work best for your company, we will implore you to give feedback daily. Why? Because if you are giving daily feedback, never will an employee be shocked or surprised when a poor performance review occurs, nor would they be surprised if they were let go and/or placed on an improvement plan. This all sounds simple enough but a key thing to remember is that giving feedback doesn't come naturally to most— it's a learned behavior that must be practiced by all and deliberately built into the culture. We will discuss this more in Chapter Eight.

Do you fire humanely and fast?

Last but not least, while we will cover termination best practices later, this point cannot be overlooked. Sometimes a situation is very cut and dry. For example, an employee who steals or shows up intoxicated for a client meeting has to go. But those cases, fortunately, are not as commonplace as dealing with an employee who is just not improving even if feedback has been given, or an improvement plan is in place. When this is the situation, don't hold off for several weeks. That can stifle morale and even give other employees the wrong idea that you are conflict adverse or lack leadership skills. Instead, pull in your HR and legal support team and quickly make the decision to let that employee go. Remember, the compassionate thing to do might just be firing that employee. Do it quickly and as humanely as possible.

Lastly, remember that these aren't easy questions to answer. Asking yourself to be honest and then implementing changed behaviors takes practice, courage, and work. You as the head of your culture must hold yourself accountable. It is your job, not HR's to establish your company's culture.

6

THE BASICS OF HIRING

So you are growing and you need to expand your team. One of the most common questions we have seen over the years from entrepreneurs and small business owners is how to hire the right talent. While a great question, the answer requires knowing why you are hiring in the first place. That might sound simple, or almost dumb, but it is often not an easy answer. Are you hiring for growth, or are you hiring to fix a problem? If you are hiring for growth, then great, your job is now to narrow the scope of the position and align that position with your strategic plans. However, if you are hiring to "fix a problem," then before you hire you must first do an analysis of how your current staff is performing. What is the problem you are trying to solve? Whose roles and responsibilities need to change? Does anyone need to be let go, or is your company just understaffed?

Again, these questions seem simple but they require you as the business owner to be brutally honest with yourself and your business. You must not only analyze your current staff's strengths and weaknesses, but also your own strengths and weaknesses. This is an important step in the process. If your company isn't running efficiently, hiring another person will likely make matters worse as it increases communication channels. Figure out what the exact problem is and what skill set your team really lacks, then be very intentional about your hire.

Creating the Job Description

The first step in hiring the right candidate is to prepare a clear job description that outlines what you're looking for in a new employee and what they can expect from the job. The structure of the job description may vary from company to company and you will want the description to somewhat reflect the culture and style of your industry and workplace.

It is a best practice to ensure that job descriptions within your organization are standardized so that they have the same appearance and fully incorporate all information that you have regarding the role/position. While you will never be able to fully capture all of the data pertinent to the role, you can get pretty close. We highly encourage adding disclaimer language to the job description so as to make it very clear that not all assigned duties are listed.

According to SHRM, the following topics should be included in all job descriptions:

- Job title—name of the position.
- Classification—exempt or nonexempt under the Fair Labor Standards Act (FLSA)
- Salary grade/level/family/range—compensation levels are important. You do not want to waste hours interviewing a candidate only to realize they require $30k more than what you are capable of paying them.
- Reports to—title of the position this job reports to.
- Date—date when the job description was written or last reviewed. Job descriptions should be updated and reviewed in established intervals.
- Summary—summary and overall objectives of the job. This is where you should insert

information on your company and culture as well.

- Essential functions—essential functions, including how an individual is to perform them and the frequency of these key activities.
- Competency—knowledge, skills and abilities. These are the traits and skills the individual must possess. For a list of competencies visit or become a member of SHRM.
- Supervisory responsibilities—direct reports, if any, and the level of supervision. Note: Including supervisory responsibilities is vital and often left off of job descriptions. If a person is a manager who has 1 report, vs a manager that has 35 reports, that greatly impacts skill requirements and pay scales.
- Work environment—the work environment; temperature, noise level, inside or outside, or other factors that will affect the person's working conditions while performing the job. This is especially important for non-office jobs.
- Physical demands—the physical demands of the job, including bending, sitting, lifting and driving. Remember, accommodations might need to be made but you as a business owner need to describe expectations.
- Position type and expected hours of work—full time or part time, typical work hours and shifts, days of week, and whether overtime is expected.

- Travel—percentage of travel time expected for the position. Where the travel happens is a nice to have (i.e. International vs. within a specific state, etc.)
- Required and preferred education and experience—education and experience based on requirements that are job-related and consistent with business necessity.
- Additional eligibility qualifications— additional requirements such as certifications, industry-specific experience and experience working with certain equipment.
- Affirmative action plan/equal employment opportunity (AAP/EEO) statement—clause(s) that outlines federal contractor requirements and practices and/or equal employer opportunity statement. Oftentimes small companies forget that EEO laws require a EEO statement. If you have more than 15 employees, this needs to be on every job description and on your recruitment site.

Now you can start customizing the job description. Remember to make the position look appealing. It is considered best practice to add a small paragraph about your company, its mission, vision, and values. Include awards. It is also important to list benefits on a job description. What does paid time off (PTO) look like? How about medical, dental, 401(k) or IRA, etc? Make your company shine! The more you can include in the job description, the less questions you will receive once you start your interview process.

Once the job description is complete, it is time to post. Make sure you advertise in a few locations in order to ensure a large enough candidate pool. Consider paying for your position to be posted on sites like Indeed and Linkedin for a specific amount of time. We suggest two weeks. The goal is well over 20 candidates for each position.

Before you Interview: Beware of the "Culture Fit"

It is not uncommon for small business owners to hire individuals with the same values and/or background as themselves. We hear it all the time when speaking to small business owners— "I am hiring X because I think they will be a good culture fit." And while this approach is intuitive to most, hiring based primarily on culture is a mistake.

Finding the right people is not a matter of "culture fit." What most people really mean when they say someone is a good fit culturally is that he or she is someone they'd like as a friend. But people from all different backgrounds can be great at the job. This misguided hiring strategy can also contribute to a company's lack of diversity. And if you as a business owner value innovation and growth, diversity of thought is a key competency you must seek out.

The company in which there is no conflict is the one where there's little innovation or thinking. The reason you need people not like you is because they will spark argument and even dissent. Yes, some workplace conflict is actually good. Coworkers who don't share worldviews, often have an increased ability to spot risks, see opportunities, or collaborate in ways that expand upon ideas and business lines. If your small company is looking to grow, you will need to seek out diversity. And while we aren't encouraging you to hire someone who absolutely won't fit in, we are encouraging you to hire people who think differently than you do.

The Interview Process

Once you have received a large enough sample of job applications, the next step is to weed out candidates that do not meet your minimum requirements. This includes pulling resumes that you are not impressed with—albeit because of massive typos and/or for being unprofessional. But before you go wild and start getting really picky, let me define unprofessional. Unprofessional at this stage isn't "I don't like the pink paper the resume is on, or the cover letter was too unpassionate." Unprofessional means red-flags.

> *We received a cover letter from a candidate that was 5 pages in length, single spaced, and discussed the individuals life-story including sexual and medical information. The oversharing was inappropriate and to the level that already broke the company's code of conduct. In a different job search we received an application from a candidate for a job in the range of 70-100k in salary where the applicant wrote they were interested but would not accept under 200k for the position. These are what you are looking to weed out.*
>
> *-Laura*

Once you have narrowed the pile to about 15-20 of your top candidates, now is the time to schedule phone interviews. Phone interviews do not need to be long. In fact, they should be less than 20 minutes. The interview is more of a screening whereby you ask specific questions about the individuals resume and experience to further narrow down the candidate list to under 10 candidates. If the screening narrows down to between 4-7 candidates, that is great! You are verifying experience during these calls and getting a sense for the level of interest by the candidate. Once you have narrowed the list of applicants, it is time for in-person and/or video conference interviews.

In advance of the job interview, you will need to prep. It is important to structure the interview in a way that is uniform. Each candidate should have an opportunity to answer the same set of questions. Of course there may be some variation due to the flow of the conversation, and it should be a conversation, not an interrogation. This is so you can cross-compare notes and rank after all have been interviewed. If the interviews are not structured in the same way, you will be unable to rank the candidates fairly.

During the actual job interview, your role is to help the candidate demonstrate their knowledge, skills, and experience. But remember, they are likely nervous. So go ahead and start with small talk and ask a few easy questions until they relax. Once relaxed, begin the interview. We suggest asking a series of behavioral questions during the interview.

Behavioral interviews are often the best tool you have to identify candidates who have the behavioral traits and characteristics that you have selected as necessary for the position. Additionally, behavioral interview questions ask the candidate to pinpoint specific instances in which a particular behavior was exhibited in the past. They include questions like:

- Tell me about a time when you obtained a new customer through networking activities and how did you close the deal?
- In your past projects what was your role, your contributions, your successes, your failures and your lessons learned?
- Give me an example of a time when you lost a client? Why did you lose them and what did you learn from the experience?
- What are your three most important work-related traits/values within the teams you have managed? What are some examples?

Once you have completed all interviews, your top two or three candidates should be fairly clear. If done correctly, you should have several candidates who you'll want to ask back for a second interview, possibly even a third interview if the job is a leadership position. Once you, and your team, have settled on your candidate, it's time to craft an offer letter and begin the negotiation process. Remember, the salary range should already have been listed on the description, your job now is to offer the candidate the amount they are worth within that range.

Background checks – Friend and Foe

Let's be honest. We have all heard those horror stories in the local news of small local companies going bankrupt because the trusted bookkeeper embezzled. Even more shocking is that in some cases if the employer had run a background check, they would have known the bookkeeper had a less than stellar history.

If you are in the service industry, or hiring any employee who will have access to your systems, it is imperative that you perform background checks. Background checks can greatly reduce the risk of a bad hire and also give you insight into the character that you will be adding to your team.

However, before you run a background check, refer to an employment attorney or reputable local screening firm. Why? Because in recent years fair hiring laws have become increasingly robust. As a result, background checks are governed by a myriad of federal, state, and local laws and regulations. For example, in some states it is illegal not to hire a convicted drug offender for certain drugs. Likewise, when it comes to being inclusive, past convictions should not be a factor in hiring unless they are related to the job at hand. For example, you wouldn't want to hire a person who committed embezzlement to manage financials, but a past DUI should not be held against that individual because driving is not in the job description. Failure to comply with federal, state and local laws can result in costly fines and lawsuits that can end up costing a company millions.

Another common mistake companies make when it comes to background checks is that employers fail to maintain the correct authorization forms. If you are not compliant, you might be breaking the law and will face fines.

To mitigate against the above mentioned examples your company should work with a trusted, accountable third party provider who can provide up-to-date forms and information for your company in a timely manner. This will greatly reduce your risk. **Make sure you understand how they track new legislation that impacts form compliance and hiring, and how they communicate these changes to their clients.**

It is important to note that consent forms should be separate from job applications and never included in a job application as they will be updated. The application will probably not be updated. Remember, it is imperative that you protect your business. That means running background checks. It also means following all laws and regulations.

I was a young new plant manager when a random question *led to the discovery that our plant controller had been embezzling funds for years. Not a lot, but just enough to go unnoticed. It was somewhat sad to see the impact his years of embezzlement had on him once the truth came to light.*

-Art

7

ONBOARDING: CREATE A PROCESS

While serial entrepreneurs might disagree, when it comes to HR the self-starter culture is overrated. By "self-starter", we mean that oftentimes business owners forget to onboard new hires because they themselves didn't require it. Remember, that is why you are the business owner. If no one needed guidance, we would all work for ourselves.

For small startups without a standalone HR department, onboarding can be a nightmare. Due to the lack of personnel, it's usually up to the founder or another leader to take the new hire under their wing for the first week. Sadly, given work demands this is often not doable, and the new hire is thrown into their job without the guidance they need. This often leads to blurred lines, resentment, and turnover.

Note: It is important to remember that SHRM estimates that turnover, on average, **costs a company one-third of the annual wages of the worker who left.**

Why? Because many small business owners, who are already overworked, don't take the time to create an onboarding plan. They take on the attitude of "nobody onboarded me, the employee can figure it out." And the task of creating a systematized onboarding plan is dropped because of time constraints or lack of delegation.

It's a vicious cycle whereby a buried and short-staffed business owner hires more employees to spread the work. And, when they don't have time to onboard or train the new hires, the new hires leave within 3-18 months from lack of feeling like they are a part of the team.

The reality is when you are disorganized with the first steps of bringing on a new team member to your company, it sets the wrong tone right out of the gate. This in turn, greatly impacts retention.

As noted by Forbes magazine, statistics have shown that 20% of all staff turnover occurs within the first 45 days of employment. This, of course, is a result of poor onboarding or a misalignment of capacity coupled with the idea that many have other job options they have been exploring.

The Benefits of Onboarding

EMPLOYER
Cost Savings
-
Lower Turnover
-
Improved
Teamwork

Better Performance
-
Organizational
Commitment
-
Lower Stress

EMPLOYEE
Higher Job
Satisfaction
-
More Career
Opportunities
-
Faster Team
Integration

So how does an employer break this self-starter habit and set their employees up for success? The following steps are a high-level overview of best practices for building out a sustainable onboarding process.

Pre-Onboarding

Most employees don't start their jobs for a few weeks after they accept a job offer. While this can delay the transfer of capacity, onboarding starts the second the offer is accepted. During "pre-onboarding" as it's often referred to, depending on your size/industry, you may have different compliance regulations to consider. But for small businesses and/or startups, the list tends to be the same. It includes setting up the new hires email address, possibly sending an employee contract, completing the Federal I9, sending over all policies and procedures like the employee handbook, and answering any questions about what to expect on the first day (what to wear, where to park, who to ask for, etc). By getting all the paperwork out of the way, this eases the administrative burden for your entire team and speeds up the ability of your new hire to jump into their role. It also gives your candidate a sense of organization on your company's end.

We recommend that you send any pre-requisite work (i.e.: drug-screens, etc.) that might be legally required for the employee to complete before their first day. Other items to consider preparing in advance include a parking pass, keys and/or badges, a desk space, computer, phone, and any other tech items needed or required for work. Use the few weeks before your hire arrives to fully prepare so that day one can be a smooth transition for all.

The First Day

As the Forbes Onboarding article confirms, first impressions can have a lasting impact. A relatively smooth first day, free of the stress of death by paperwork can go a long way to creating a great experience. There are always a lot of variables, so it is best to be flexible, particularly early on when you are still figuring all of this out. The goal isn't to have 100 percent of the paperwork completed by the first day, but to have the vast majority of it completed. Give the new team member a clear expectation and timeline for the completion of any remaining paperwork.

While you do want to ensure all legally required information and paperwork are complete, the first day is really about getting to know your new team member, introducing them to the rest of the team, and making them feel at ease. Be prepared to greet your new hire. This might seem obvious, but what we mean is to be prepared to physically greet them when they walk in the door. Get there before they do and be waiting. Give the appearance you are prepared for the day, and don't let them stumble into the office unsure where to report. It sets the tone, definitely of the day and maybe of their time with you.

If you have a business reason that you as the business owner cannot be there to greet the new hire, delegate this key activity to someone else in the office. Make sure this team member understands the importance of making the new team member feel at ease and helping them settle in. Communicate with both the new team member and their onboarding mentor as soon as possible to help set the tone and teamwork dynamic.

Upon entering into the office, it is also a great idea to have prepped their desk in advance (have it clean) and to leave some kind of welcoming package, company swag, and/or gift. Even if it's a bagel and coffee, have something that is waiting for them that says "we are so excited that you are here." Next to the swag, have a pre-planned employee agenda that includes both the first day and week's activities. We suggest a very detailed agenda for day one, and a somewhat detailed agenda for the rest of the week. Don't let the new employee sit at their desk waiting for tasks to be sent over, instead integrate them into everyone's work week.

We often recommend having the employee shadow anyone who will be reporting to them, or who they will be reporting to for a few hours each day to get to know them, to learn systems (time-tracking, intranet, project management, CRMs, etc.), and to set expectations. Make sure every employee scheduled to meet with the new hire that week is tasked with teaching the new hire something pertinent to their new role. Hold all accountable for this onboarding process and allow for back-up support for those who are assisting with this onboarding process. For example, if a new hire needs to spend 10 hours shadowing another employee, find someone who can assist with their projects and deliverables so as to not overwhelm them or derail deliverables. This not only builds camaraderie, but makes all feel valued. You know you're off to a good start when you get the impression that everyone pitches in, works together and grows and sacrifices as a team. For those team members who usually make great impacts there is very little that is more exciting.

Lastly, sometime during the first week, arrange a team welcome lunch or happy hour to welcome the new hire. Make sure that someone on the team takes the new team member to lunch on their first day. Nothing builds rapport faster than breaking bread. This can be simple—pizza or subs or a morning coffee break. It's about the welcome and the intent. It doesn't have to be expensive but it does have to be authentic. Make it a part of your culture.

Systemize this process for ease. This will probably not be the only hire that you ever have. Create an internal task list for all the items so this process is easily duplicated for the next hire, and that each team member knows their role in the onboarding process, with due dates and who can assist them with support.

First Two Weeks

During the first two weeks, schedule a few check in meetings to touch base with the new hire and see how they are doing. It gives you a chance to monitor them a little closer early on and build a rapport, as well as it gives them the chance to ask any questions that they may have. These do not need to be long, but serve to answer questions about responsibilities and anything that might be unclear about their role or the systems you have in place.

Your role as the business owner is to paint a big picture for what the new hires' duties include and why. Before handing over large projects or tasks, help the new hire understand the strategic importance of what you are asking. Make sure that you also cover what is important to you as a business owner, and what you expect of that employee.

Use this time with the new hire to review the mission, vision, company values. This should truly be a review and not the first time that these key points have been shared with the new team member. These two week check-ins do not have to be formal although they should be slightly more organized than on the spot check-ins, conversations and interactions that you have had with them every few days.

Once you're comfortable that the high-level overview stuff is adequately covered, it is time to get tactical. That is when to slowly (yes slowly) begin to hand over tasks, projects, and responsibilities to the new hire to manage. Depending on the role and size of the organization, it can take several weeks for an employee to become fully integrated into their position.

Taking business considerations into perspective, your job as their new boss is to not overwhelm them. You want to phase them in to the projects and workload, not dump it on them day one. This is a delicate balance because you did hire them to contribute. Their contribution over the long-term will be much more if they are not overwhelmed or over burdened while they are still trying to figure out some of the basics of working with the new team. You have to know when to push and when to let up so that they can find their own rhythm and excel.

30-60-90

The first two weeks are the most important when it comes to onboarding, but the onboarding process does not end after the first two weeks. With some exceptions, onboarding programs should run anywhere between 30-90 days. 90 days often being the most common that many small to medium size companies choose to end their onboarding program.

Some small companies even contractually bring talent in under a 90-day probationary period whereby if anything goes sideways during the employee's first 90 days, the company has the right to terminate without reason or severance. Probationary best practices and rules are often dependent upon the state and job type. Ask your employment lawyer the best way to establish a probationary period.

Much like the first two weeks, the first 30 days of a new hire's onboarding should include learning company-specific platforms, policies, the team, and the ins and outs of their role. This could include starting project work, or taking training required for their work.

The second month of employment (60 days) should focus more on collaboration and taking on more responsibilities and duties. Important goals for the 60 days include regular meetings with their manager and establishing metrics for feedback for the employee's performance. This is also the time for the new employee to raise concerns or pain points so that leadership can act quickly to address. As the manager, be proactive in asking the new hire about their concerns. Don't assume there are none if none are raised.

And finally, the last 90 days, or third month of employment, is when the training wheels come off. As the employee starts taking on more responsibilities, 60-90 days is when full accountability is established, and a more standardized approach to meetings and communication should occur.

If your company is large enough to have key performance indicators (KPIs) they should begin to be applied during this time period. In other words, the new team member should be fully integrated into the company, team and business systems and processes and is now responsible for the numbers/goals that have been established for their role and responsibilities. They are no longer the new kid. They should understand the expectations associated with their role.

Your company's 30-60-90 program should be systemized for ease and consistency. Every employee, manager, and new hire should know what is expected of them. Every phase of your onboarding process should be focused on goals that build and support your strategy. This is how you as a leader best position your new hires to become successful team members. And remember, your onboarding process is a living process. Continue to refine it as your company grows.

8

CULTURE IS KEY

The way that your team relates to your customers and each other, and the way that they problem solve, typically defines the culture of small teams. Your main charge, as the leader, is to make sure that the values and ethics of the organization are upheld in all decision making and actions. This, in a nutshell, defines your culture.

Your team knows when you value their input. They feel when they have the freedom to openly and honestly contribute. They also feel when their contributions are not valued. People are naturally more open and productive when they are being heard. A team of collaborative contributors is one of the most potent things a company can have.

Great cultures are built on communication. Communication is not a one-way street. In today's world it is a multi-lane highway. Communication must flow…in real time…from your team members to customers…to each other…to leaders…to 3rd party support…and just about any combination of these. People have to know that they can trust the information that they receive.

Be honest in all of your communications with the team and your customers…even when it hurts. Authenticity in communications builds trust and trust builds value.

9

Avoiding Favorites

One of the reasons individuals are motivated to start a business is so that they can have more control over their lives. That may include the people that they spend the most of their time with: their coworkers. No one prefers working with jerks. Most people prefer to work with people that they like.

This can start out innocent enough, but it can, once the team grows, begin to morph into favoritism. The problem with favoritism is that it doesn't have to be persistent, it actually doesn't have to be real, it can just be perceived. That one small perception, or misperception is like a virus. It can gnaw at the trust and relationships that you have carefully crafted, divide your team, and cause legal challenges and damages.

Whatever you do as a leader, be fair and equitable to all, even the people that you like less than others. Impartiality is a key characteristic of a strong leader. Strong leaders tend to build strong teams. Strong teams tend to succeed. Do not show favorites.

A nasty step child of favoritism is office politics. People typically use office politics to gain favor or recognition with leadership. At best this creates tension in the work environment. At worse it can spawn open conflict among team members and lead to lost work efficiencies.

I once worked with a founder who very unintentionally showed massive amounts of favoritism. While everyone else in the office would be scolded for misplacing equipment, or for a small error, there was one individual who was never scolded. In fact, this individual received all the praise, even if it was for someone else's work, and they also received all the awards. Never once was this individual told they were making mistakes when they were. While not the founder's intention, their actions led to several individuals quitting, especially female employees, who felt they could not live up to the standards created. Given the fact that females were the ones leaving, this led to possible issues and concerns around discrimination *and required legal council's assistance— all because the founder preferred working with one individual.*

-Laura

10

TALENT MANAGEMENT BASICS

As mentioned earlier in the book, HR plays many roles within a company, but of those roles few are as all encompassing as talent management and development. This is because talent management is not just learning and development, but includes your organization's entire strategy as it relates to the attraction, recruitment, retention, and development of your employees. It includes your recruiting processes, onboarding, performance review, learning development, and even succession planning.

We covered onboarding and hiring, but talent management is a lot more than just that. Managing

HR procedures and processes are not synonymous with talent management. You need a talent management strategy—one that is designed for your company in alignment with your strategic plan. Why is this important? For starters, because it's ten times harder to reach your business goals with the wrong people.

The ability to sustain a steady supply of critical talent is a challenge facing all organizations — worldwide — large or small. While a small company can get away with not formalizing a lot of HR processes, skipping on talent development will absolutely guarantee high turnover and maybe even the collapse of your company.

> *I invested in a small construction company that was performing government contracts. Unfortunately, we put the wrong leadership in place and the company slowly eroded away. We were able to prevent any major financial challenges, but it took several years to clean up the mess that poor leadership, and even worse results left behind.*
>
> *-Art*

The hardest part is that no one person or book can tell you exactly what will be required in order to develop your talent management plan. The plan is dependent not only on the industry and state you are in, but also on the organizational structure that you have. For example, is your organization flat, matrixed, or chain-of-command? What state regulations does your industry have? What does compensation within your industry look like? What values and ethics do you want all your employees trained on? The questions are endless.

Talent management is focused on your long-term strategy, as opposed to the day-to-day transactional nature of most topics in HR. It requires asking big, tough questions and there is no one-size-fits-all blueprint for success. The only advice we can give you is to invest in talent management, do not be afraid of change, test different processes and formats, and measure, measure, and measure again to see if you are on the right track. In the meantime, we will start with the basics: Annual reviews and growth opportunities; and the importance of building a feedback culture.

Annual reviews and growth opportunities

Let's start with the dreaded annual review. We say dreaded because nobody likes annual reviews—neither the manager who has to fill them out, nor the employee that receives the feedback. But, if done correctly, annual reviews go from being merely necessary to being absolutely beneficial to all parties. Employees deserve to know what the organization and their leaders think of them, and this process ensures that even poor managers are required to give feedback to their employees and are held accountable for their management skills.

Without boring you to tears, the history behind performance reviews and best practices, has been a 100 year conversation that actually began during World War I when the US military started a merit system to rank the performance of their soldiers. By the 1950s and 1960s, as a result of many wars, most US companies had adopted a ranking system for performance whereby once a year you were ranked against your coworkers, and based on your ranking your salary was adjusted or you were placed on an improvement plan. In fact, many governmental organizations continue the ranking practice to this day, with companies like GE only having stopped ranking employees in the early 2000s.

As a small business owner we highly advise against the creation of a ranking and/or merit system. Forced ranking fosters internal competition and will undermine collaboration amongst small teams. Instead, create a culture of feedback whereby feedback on performance is given in real time and the annual review is simply a review of the year's feedback and a conversation on growth goals.

Things the employee should be measured on should reflect the values of your organizational culture. Principles like collaboration, self-organization, self-direction, inclusion, and how the employee can work more efficiently or with agility should be the focus. Employees should be benchmarked against their own performance and growth goals and not the goals of their co-workers. The format of the review can be as simple as a handwritten questionnaire or the use of a digital performance review platform. Choose what is easiest and most secure for your organization.

No one size fits all when it comes to performance management so please know this is not exhaustive. However, here are a few questions and areas to cover during the annual review:

- **Job description goals.** These are goals based on the achievement of a pre-established set of job duties from the individual's job description. These goals are expected to be accomplished continuously until the job description changes. Examples might be financial sales goals, customer feedback, or process- and system-oriented goals.

- **Project goals.** These are goals based on the achievement of project objectives. These goals may be set for a single year and changed as projects are completed. The job description and project goals are "what" needs to be accomplished by the employee in order to stay employed.

- **Behavioral goals.** Goals may be based on certain behaviors. These goals are expected to be accomplished continuously as well. They are "how" things need to be accomplished. This is where your mission, vision, and values come into play. For example, if inclusivity is an important company value, then every employee should be measured on inclusivity within this section of the performance review.

- **Stretch goals.** Last but not least, stretch goals should be established for each employee. These include skill building activities or additional duties that are established in order to expand the knowledge, skills and abilities of high-potential employees, and to keep engagement high.

Source: https://www.shrm.org/resourcesandtools/tools-and-samples/toolkits/pages/managingemployeeperformance.aspx

Lastly, it is imperative that the employee, before seeing the feedback of their manager, fills out a self-review of their own performance. Why you ask?

Because this is where management/HR establishes alignment.

Once reviews are finished, the employee and the manager should send a copy of their reviews to HR, or you as the business owner, before meeting to hold the actual review. If there are massive discrepancies between the manager's review and the employee's review, one of two issues has occurred—either the manager is failing to give feedback and guidance to the employee, or the employee's goals are not in alignment with the company. Either way, corrective actions will be needed by upper management and/or HR as salary increases should, in part, be dependent on performance. This leads us to our next section on the importance of building a feedback culture

The importance of a feedback culture

Annual reviews should simply be a part of a greater feedback process that is continuous and timely and flows throughout the entire year. This way employees know how they are doing and what is expected. There should not be discrepancies or surprises during performance reviews. That said, we would be grossly misleading you if we didn't, at a minimum, discuss what giving feedback means.

There have been a lot, and we mean a lot, of books written on the importance of giving feedback and how to do it well. While we are not covering all of that in this book, we do recommend reviewing various approaches to giving feedback as it offers a great deal of insight into how to have tough and amazing workplace conversations. But before we move on to the next chapter, we must establish what feedback is.

Feedback does not mean focusing on the shortcomings of your employees. It is the exact opposite of that. Focusing on shortcomings minimizes an employee's confidence and hinders their ability to learn.

Instead, feedback should be focused on systemizing praise and dissecting things you as the business owner see that are working. For example, after a project occurs, don't tell the employee what went wrong and how to fix it. Instead say, "here are two-three things that really worked for me, and two-three that didn't." This gives the employee immediate praise and constructive feedback, but it also clearly establishes your expectations. Additionally, this format is outcome based versus a personal attack on the team member.

Feedback should be specific and very tactical in nature. As a manager, don't say "You need to work on your communications skills" because the employee has no idea what part of their communication is broken and therefore they do not know how to address it. Instead, say something along the lines of "Here is the exact moment when I got lost in the conversation" or "the communication broke down at X moment, how might we fix that in the future?"

I remember some of the worst feedback I ever received from a manager. I was 25 years old and the manager, who was also the CEO of the company, took me out to coffee to tell me that while my performance was excellent, all revenue goals had been met and the clients were all happy, she would not be giving me the promotion to Consultant from Associate Consultant because I really needed to work on being more 'zen'. I was a bit dumbfounded and asked the CEO what they meant. To which they responded, "have you tried meditation or yoga?" There was no example given for being zen, not even an explanation for the behavior that was the issue being addressed. I left that organization about ten months later frustrated by my lack of career path and understanding of goals. Fast-forward several years later and I am having a coffee with a former co-worker from that company. We both were discussing the odd feedback that we received while working at the firm.

When I told my story about not being promoted due to my lack of zen, my co-worker said "Oh, I remember you were one of the highest performing employees we had, it was just you didn't prioritize the projects and workloads of others. You were so driven to be successful with your own accounts you didn't understand the needs of the support staff." And at that moment I knew exactly what the feedback was. Had I understood before, it could have been corrected. Moral of the story, as a small business owner, learn to give highly specific, and outcome-based feedback. This is the only way you will establish a culture that fosters the development and engagement of your team.

-Laura

11

WHEN YOU HAVE TO DOWNSIZE OR LET GO

In one of our previous books, "Making Your Business Thrive in a Recession" we discussed downsizing, terminations, and off-boarding a great deal. While we will not re-review furlough best practices or financial considerations when it comes to managing in a business down cycle, that requires reading the book, we will review best practices when it comes to letting people go.

All businesses expand and contract. When a business contracts or business needs change, sometimes you have to change people. This is natural and this is hard. It is really hard when you have a small team and have known and worked with people for years. Even worse is if you consider your employee a friend. Be thankful for the memories, be humane in how you address the situation, acknowledge the difficult feelings — both theirs and yours — and make the decision to do the hard but right thing and move forward.

Downsizing and/or financial hardships are never easy on anyone within an organization. This is why communication is key. Don't let the first communication with your team be the worst news possible, or worse still, the last communication you have with them before they are let go. The memories of how you handled hard HR decisions will be remembered by all. Be open and honest every step of the process. Even when emotions are high, you will be able to sleep knowing you did everything in your power to calm fears and steady the ship.

Create a Downsizing Plan

To start, you as the leader must decide what is, and is not, financially feasible. This is not an easy decision as many people will be impacted. Don't wait until cash runs out. The minute you recognize that there is a need to make cuts, act, and act fast. This will be key to keeping the lights on, and possibly saving the maximum number of jobs.

If it is apparent that lay-offs are needed, the first thing that must be considered is how to consolidate redundancies within the organization. i.e.: Can the job of two workers be performed by one? Is job-sharing an appropriate option, or will it break the morale and productivity of the team? Can any of your employees be moved into new, more essential roles? While layoffs are never ideal for morale, they can be necessary for your company's long-term business survival. If your company is struggling financially, you absolutely cannot afford to pay for repetitive processes. Just like you would create a growth plan, you need to make a plan for downsizing.

Call in the Professionals

State laws vary, and the number of employees in your organization affects what laws regarding employee termination apply to your business. Check first with your employment attorney to ensure that your approach is compliant. Take into consideration any resources you may need to provide your employee upon termination. Then as you begin to build out your downsizing plan, bring in HR to ensure that you don't miss anything.

Ignorance, though often argued, is not a defense in court. Spend the time and money, even when money is tight, to learn what you need to do in order to let people go in a fair, ethical and legal manner. A wrongful termination or discrimination lawsuit does not add value to your business or your life. If you only take one piece of advice from this chapter, it is to call your lawyer. Avoiding a few legal fees on the front end could cost you a significant amount of money, time and energy later.

In addition to ensuring you are compliant, HR and legal counsel can assist you in dealing with the many questions your employees will have if they are terminated. For example, if you provide health insurance benefits, you will be responsible for offering COBRA continuation coverage in many situations. You will want to know, going into each termination or furlough conversation, exactly what benefits each employee is eligible for. COBRA can be complicated. Mistakes are easy to make and can include everything from miscalculating coverage periods, to not properly counting your employees, to failing to also consider state laws (not just federal laws), and more. You will need HR and legal guidance to ensure you are both compliant, and equitably meeting the needs of your employees.

Additional questions that your legal counsel and/or an HR advisor can assist you with, and that you need to deal with long before communicating your downsizing plan with your employees, include:

- What does your HR handbook say? Before making layoffs, you will need to determine if there has been any formal or informal severance plan or policy, even if it was in precedent, for benefits you might need to offer your terminated employees.

- What are the 401(k), IRA, and other retirement plan implications? If your company offers FTEs (full time equivalents) retirement benefits, work closely with your HR team, benefit advisors and broker to determine how this will impact your communications with the impacted employees. It is important to note that a furlough might qualify as a "partial termination" under some retirement plans, which triggers 100 percent vesting for the furloughed employees. You won't know until you have spoken to all parties how your plan will impact your employees.

- In the case of the termination of an executive, how does this affect any deferred compensation agreements, stock or ghost stock agreements, and other benefits? If money is owed to an employee, work with legal and HR to determine a fair and equitable payment plan that you can propose to the employee during the termination meeting.

- How will unused Paid Time Off be resolved? Again, check with your lawyer. Many states require vacation payouts upon termination. This might also be addressed in your handbook. Review each employee's case with HR and determine how to address this during the termination meeting with the employee.

Prepare for Terminations

If you are a small company, it is possible that you will be handling the layoffs yourself. If this is the case, this means you are the manager and you will need to come up with your own communication plan for each employee. A mass announcement might not be needed unless a few cuts have to be made. If this is the case, go ahead and schedule back to back meetings with the employees you need to let go. And, once the employees have been let go, schedule a team meeting with the remaining staff to explain the changes.

However, for a slightly larger organization, you might have a management team or several dozens of employees. If this is the case, the managers will first need to be informed if any of their team members are being laid off. Assuming none of the managers are impacted by the layoffs, your first step is to schedule a private announcement with the manager(s) an hour or so before sitting down with the employees that will be let go. A short timeline limits the spread of rumors. Rumors can hurt morale, and usually leads to confusion and miscommunication. If word were to leak in even one email, your credibility as a leader will be questioned. It is imperative to control the narrative.

Once managers have been informed, it is time to communicate via a formal announcement regarding the plan to downsize. Explain the reasons for the upcoming layoffs, the scope of the changes, and the long-term plan for recovery. Do not sugar coat or apologize. And most importantly, acknowledge that people may be feeling nervous about how layoff decisions are being made. This is normal. Let your employees know that this is normal, and then clearly communicate. While often emotional, steadfast leadership is required during this time. Reiterate how carefully you have explored all options. There is no alternative but to make cuts.

Once the announcement is made, work with managers to schedule one-on-ones with their team members who are being let go first, and then with those employees whose roles are being impacted.

Remember, people are nervous and will want reassurance. Employees taking on additional responsibilities will need to feel heard, and to fully understand what their work now looks like given the organizational restructuring.

The Termination Meeting

With all the hard decisions that you have to make, as a leader you also have to manage the emotional needs of your team members in the organization. There is a right way—with empathy, compassion, and understanding—to let someone go so that they can keep their dignity and respect. It requires time, energy, forethought and the willingness to listen and show empathy while exercising your resolve. There are right ways to do this but unfortunately, there are many, many examples, in all business sectors, of the wrong way to do this.

While many in HR will give you advice on how to effectively hold a termination meeting with an employee, layoffs are slightly different. Remember, you aren't terminating an employee for poor performance or bad conduct. This is purely a long-term business sustainability decision. As you have established your reasons earlier in your business-wide communication, now you must do it individually. Do not make excuses. Be fair and be resolute.

As you prepare for your meeting, remember to dot every "i" and cross every "t". Make sure you have spoken with all benefits brokers, legal counsel, HR and payroll. Have a script pre-planned to ensure you cover all bases, and accept the possibility that the employee will become frustrated, emotional, or angry. This is normal. Do not personalize their emotions. Your job is to give them all relevant information, and to ensure them that this has been thought through.

If you believe a termination meeting might be emotional, or worse, if the meeting involves a problem employee, or an employee who has previously made discrimination or harassment claims, make sure you bring another manager (never a coworker) or HR professional to the termination meeting. Having someone else present can help diffuse a bad situation and give you a witness who can attest to what was said and done.

The other reason to have a witness is due to the increasing number of employees who falsely accuse managers of harassment, retaliation and other illegal behaviors in an effort to file a claim or keep their job. Since 2000, the number of claims filed each year with the EEOC has almost doubled. A neutral third-party witness can make a big difference in the event that the employee files a false claim.

As you open the meeting up, start by thanking the employee for their service to the company, all they have done, and how hard this decision is. Then inform them of the decision. Be prepared to explain why, but under no circumstances debate the decision. You aren't going to convince the employee if they begin to debate you. Let them be emotional, but do not waste time. Turn the conversation to immediate next steps and the things to which the employee is entitled.

Build in an Exit Interview

Typically, exit interviews are conducted by an HR practitioner with an employee who voluntarily quits a job. The employee exit interview feedback is used to assist HR and leadership to determine organizational improvements and what groups or managers might need support. During layoffs, the employee is not leaving willfully. They are being let go for reasons outside of their control. While not necessary, the end of a termination meeting should still take on the feel of an exit interview. This time, in a somewhat reversed fashion. Allow the terminated employee to ask you questions, while you also arm the employee with helpful information. This might be the last time you ever see this employee. It is important that the termination meeting be managed with care.

The first topic that should be discussed with the employee is severance pay. While many small businesses may not be in the financial position to offer this, if there is any way to do so, we encourage you to try. Severance pay serves two key functions. For starters, it helps employees get back on their feet. But the second, and arguably just as important reason, is that severance pay helps deter employees from suing you for wrongful dismissal. Why? Because severance pay is not legally required. It is a sign of good faith on your part and can go a long way in protecting your trade secrets.

The second topic that should be covered in the exit interview/termination meeting is reference letters. Since your employee will be seeking work almost immediately, you will need to determine the method for handling calls from prospective employers and references. To assist the employee's job search, and reinforce your loyalty to the employee, determine an approach. As much as you can, offer to assist the employee with next steps. Since in this case the employee was terminated for reasons that are not their fault, it will be much easier to provide a good reference or a recommendation.

Finally, the last, and possibly most important conversation to hold during the exit interview/termination meeting is the employee's benefits and the return of all company property. At this point you and your legal and HR team have worked to develop benefits, health insurance, 401K policies, profit sharing and payments that need to be rolled over.

It is the employee's right to know these things upon termination. Even if you have very little to offer the employee, explain this to them and the reason why. For example, if an employee had not yet worked a certain number of months, they may not be eligible for vacation time, etc. Providing a clear picture as to what the employee is or is not getting, helps clear up misunderstandings and allows the employee to ask questions and to feel heard.

Working with legal counsel and HR, create an off-boarding checklist for all terminated employees. With all that is going on, the last thing you need to worry about is if you remembered to collect keys or parking passes from recently separated emotional employees. This list will need to be customized to include all benefits and severance package information. Additionally, you will want to work with IT or your Office Manager, to ensure that the checklist is completed on the employee's last day. This is by no means an exhaustive list. Work with HR and legal to build out a list that is unique to both your company and to the employee's role and position. For additional lists and best practices, find free downloadable checklists, sample termination letters and more from https://www.shrm.org/.

Sample Termination Checklist

To Do:

- ☐ Disable e-mail account and/or email forwarding.
- ☐ Remove employee's name, email, and picture, from email group distribution lists; internal/office phone lists, the company website, marketing collateral and directories.
- ☐ Disable employee access to all software and/or IP (This might include project management systems, CRMs, financial management software programs, chat programs, Google Drive, Asset management software, and servers)
- ☐ Disable computer access
- ☐ Disable phone extension
- ☐ Disable voicemail
- ☐ Disable security codes and passwords
- ☐ Change office mailbox
- ☐ Clean work area and remove personal belongings

Collect the following items:

- ☐ Keys:
  - ☐ Office
  - ☐ Building
  - ☐ Desk
  - ☐ File Cabinets
  - ☐ Other
- ☐ ID cards
- ☐ Building access cards
- ☐ Business cards
- ☐ Physical IP such as SOPs and files
- ☐ Nameplate
- ☐ Name badge
- ☐ Company cell phone
- ☐ Laptop
- ☐ Uniforms, hardhats, office equipment
- ☐ Tools

12

Disruption in the Office. Now what?

While we have discussed how to terminate an employee, we have not discussed how to deal with a problem employee. There are hundreds of legal and ethical reasons one might have to terminate an employee. Those can range from failing to perform one's duties, to breaking the code of conduct, or worse still, illegal behavior.

Terminating an employee because of misconduct, while unpleasant and requiring legal counsel, can be fairly cut and dry. As the leader, you document the incident from start to finish— evidence gathering as we call it— you present it to HR and then possibly have your legal counsel review it all. Then schedule the termination meeting where you present the documented evidence and terminate the employee. In this case, as we have already stated, it is best practice to have a witness present during the exchange. However, rarely is a termination this cut and dry.

There are a wide range of behaviors exhibited by employees that can create risks that impact employee engagement or even the efficiency of the business, but do not rise to the level of breaking a code of conduct or documented policy. Some general categories include gossiping, hostile tones, rude and disrespectful behavior or conversations, mild insubordination, laziness, and poor performance. So, what is to be done?

There is a fine line that business owners and HR departments must walk when it comes to managing office disruption. If you are too weak in your approach, employee morale will suffer and your reputation as a leader will be impacted. On the other hand, if you terminate too quickly, you can be seen as unfair and that can cause fear and mistrust among your employees.

Your best bet is to have a strong HR handbook that will guide your response, and to address each case quickly and in a very intentional manner. "Quickly" is key because it is not uncommon for managers or co-workers to be unwilling to intervene or complain about a disruptive colleague. Co-workers may fear retribution or that the negative behaviors will intensify if they speak up, while managers often take a "maybe this will deal with itself" approach. That couldn't be further from the truth as often the behaviors get worse when they go uncorrected. This type of leadership is tough, but it will not get any easier with time.

It is even more challenging when the problem employee is a high performer or when the team is already short-staffed. Rationalizing this behavior only makes things worse. We can't say this loud enough, this should not be the approach your organization takes!

Keeping a toxic high-performing employee is never, ever an excuse for not addressing a problem. Toxic behavior should not be allowed in the workplace and must be addressed as soon as it is identified. Toxic behavior is viral and all it does is create a caustic environment that can not perform at its peak.

When addressing workplace issues, we have a very basic approach that, while not perfect, is the minimum that business owners need to follow in order to address problematic behaviors. That process is document, train, address.

Documenting Employee Behavior

It's no secret that documenting employee behavior is hard. Sometimes you are reluctant to document something because it seems insignificant. Sometimes you don't document problematic behavior or actions because it is a hassle. Sometimes you are reluctant to document because you don't think that is normal behavior for this team member and you're sure it won't happen again. Whatever the reason, not documenting behavior, good and bad, can be a mistake. Appropriate and consistent behavior should be a part of all performance reviews.

Addressing problematic or inappropriate behaviors should be done as close to the incident, in a private setting, as possible. No one gains by publicly humiliating someone. And as we already stated, don't wait for performance reviews to address toxic behaviors, though these incidents or attitudes should be reviewed for their impact on the employee's review.

It is important to document each occurrence. This documentation will be indispensable if there is a need to terminate the employee. The documentation trail will be clear and supportive of your decision. Countless wrongful termination lawsuits have been lost because the company did not have adequate documentation.

Even if all other job goals are being met, a disruptive employee displaying toxic behaviors that go against the company's policies and values should be terminated if they fail to correct their actions. Just as you would document and terminate an employee who showed up at a client site intoxicated and endangered the lives of others, toxic behavior must be addressed head on.

Failure to address inappropriate behavior negatively impacts the rest of the team. It also may expose the company to some type of liability. As much as possible team members should be put on a path of discovery where they can learn and modify their behavior. Depending on the type and severity of the incident, this may not be possible.

Train

Training is necessary but not sufficient. Train your staff so that they understand the behavioral expectations. Basic training modules that cover different topics include people management, conflict resolution, anti-discrimination and anti-harassment. These training sessions help arm managers with the necessary skills, tools and network to address toxic workplace behaviors, as well as to provide the company adequate documentation support if a hostile work environment claim is ever filed. Facilitating meaningful teamwork activities can also build better understanding between co-workers as various personality styles, traits, and approaches to conflict are discussed in a collaborative way.

When it becomes apparent as a business owner that toxic behaviors are occurring in the workplace, HR should be notified and a training that addresses these behaviors should be developed, deployed, and built into the company's onboarding processes. Accountability must also be addressed. Your training system may constantly evolve as new challenges arise. For this reason, make sure that you select or develop a system that is flexible and can be built on with minimal disruption.

How to Address and Confront an Employee

And lastly, employees should be told the specific consequences for failure to improve upon their behaviors. Do not mince words, and document what is said. Say it in person first, then follow-up via email with a summary of what was discussed and place that correspondence within the employee's file. Mincing words or speaking in generalities to avoid discomfort is unfair to the employee who will be shocked if you eventually end up firing them.

Consistency and fairness in the treatment of all employees is important to both the morale of the team and the prevention of legal challenges. When counseling an employee this consistency and fairness is even more important. **Address the employee's behavior, not the employee themselves.**

Be clear about why the described behavior is toxic and clearly communicate your future expectations. Discuss next steps. Establish an improvement plan with the employee if warranted. This improvement plan should include scheduled check-ins to monitor progress and attitude. When you as a leader communicate clear expectations, and take quick and appropriate actions, your company will be better able to differentiate between acceptable and unacceptable behavior. That in turn minimizes the amount of drama in the workplace and allows your team to focus their energy on thriving not surviving.

13

The Small Business Guide to Compliance

Let's face it, nobody gets excited about compliance. It's boring. And if you mess it up, it can cost you millions. Worse still, regulations are ever changing. As a business owner, not only do you have to keep your finger on the pulse of multiple federal agencies' requirements, you must also track changes at the state and local levels. If you are located in multiple states, this can feel absolutely burdensome.

While no book can cover all state specific laws, the following chapter will provide a crash course in HR compliance basics that every business owner needs to understand. More importantly, it will demonstrate why having a trusted small business lawyer, in conjunction with an HR professional, is paramount to keeping your business compliant and safe. HR professionals and your legal counsel are the absolute front line of defense for a company and will help to ensure you treat people fairly, while keeping the business out of danger.

Crash Course Compliance Lesson # 1:

Employee Classification Is Hard

Of all the places we see errors, misclassifying employees is possibly the biggest mistake small businesses make. To start, small businesses have different obligations when it comes to an employee versus an independent contractor. For example, you must withhold federal and state taxes from an employee's paycheck and file a W-2 for an employee at the end of the year. When it comes to contractors, you don't usually have to withhold taxes from their pay, but you will need to submit a 1099-MISC for them at tax time.

To meet these different requirements, you must classify your team members correctly.

Unfortunately, there's no set definition of "contractor," which can make this difficult, but many states have strict laws on what is and is not a contractor. For example, if you create a title, business card, and set-up an email address for one of your 1099s, this could be a no-no. And, if your company ever undergoes a labor audit, you could face penalties and back pay to that contractor as well as back taxes based on the misclassification.

To help determine a worker's status, examine these three high-level aspects of your relationship:

1. **Behavioral control:** If you have the right to control your worker's behavior, they're likely an employee and not a contractor. For example, if you have a start and stop time or work schedule for the individual, and if you are requiring the person to use your internal systems, then this individual is a part-time employee versus a 1099.

2. **Financial control:** If you pay the person per project and don't reimburse them for job-related expenses, they're probably an independent contractor. However, if you reimburse them and the workload is fairly stable, they are an employee.

3. **Length and Benefits:** If the relationship will last indefinitely or you offer benefits, they are an employee.

Some states are making the definition of "contractor" more stringent. For example, in states like California, a person must actually be in business for themselves in order to be considered a true contractor. Ask your employment attorney for the specifics.

Once you have determined if an individual is, in fact, an employee, you must then determine whether they are exempt or non-exempt. Exempt employees do not require overtime pay. Non-exempt employees DO require overtime pay. Again, if an employee is labeled incorrectly, your company could be at risk of fines and will owe back-pay to each employee who was incorrectly classified.

You may think that these distinctions are simple, however the courts are full of cases addressing these issues every year. It doesn't matter how large or small you are. Even unicorn companies that have changed the way we look at industries, such as Uber and Lyft, have been challenged with these types of misinterpretations.

At its simplest level, a worker is exempt from overtime if they meet all of the following criteria:

- They are paid on a salary basis and they make at least $35,568 per year or $684 per week. Please note that this rate changes regularly and some states enforce more stringent requirements.

- They perform exempt job duties, such as supervising two or more people.

For all others, you will likely need to pay at least 1.5 times their hourly rate for any time worked over 40 hours in a single work week. If any of your employees are exempt from overtime but earn less than the above range, start monitoring how many hours they typically work. If they often work overtime, you will need to either increase their salary, improve their time management or productivity, or hire someone else to share their workload.

Time should be tracked to ensure you are accurately paying your employees. For more information on the FLSA (Fair Labor Standards Act) please visit the Department of Labor at https://www.dol.gov/agencies/whd/flsa.

Crash Course Compliance Lesson #2:

Know Your Medical Coverage Requirements

There have been so many changes to healthcare in the last 10 years that it is hard to keep up. Most recently, the tax penalty for not having health insurance was eliminated. However, under the Affordable Care Act (ACA), employers with 50 or more full-time equivalent employees (FTE) must provide health insurance. **As in it is Mandatory.**

Please note that an FTE (Full Time Employee) is anyone who works an average of 30 hours or more per week. Realizing this is a massive financial burden for small businesses, the punishment for not providing medical coverage is worse. In fact, if you don't provide minimum coverage to eligible workers and one of them receives a premium tax credit, you might have to pay $2,000 per person in wages. And if your plan doesn't meet the minimum coverage requirements set, as determined by ACA, you could owe $3,000 for every employee who received a premium tax credit. Know your requirements, and speak with a benefits consultant who can assist you in navigating your options.

Crash Course Compliance Lesson #3:

Know What FMLA Is, And When You Need It.

The Family and Medical Leave Act (FMLA) provides a means for employees to balance their work and family responsibilities by legally requiring companies to provide unpaid, job-protected leave for certain reasons. The Act is intended to promote the stability and economic security of families and can include reasons like illness, caretaking, and even extended maternity leave for health reasons.

The FMLA applies to any employer in the private sector who has 50 or more employees each working day during at least 20 calendar weeks in the current or preceding calendar year. The law also covers all public agencies (state and local governments) and local education agencies (schools, whether public or private). These employers do not need to meet the "50 employee" test. The Act requires employers to provide up to 12 weeks of unpaid, job-protected time off for specified family and medical reasons.

To be eligible for FMLA leave, an individual must meet the following criteria:

- Be employed by a covered employer and work at a worksite within 75 miles of which that employer employs at least 50 people;

- Have worked at least 12 months (which do not have to be consecutive) for the employer; and

- Have worked at least 1,250 hours during the 12 months immediately before the date FMLA leave is to begin.

While companies with under 50 employees are not subject to the FMLA, once financially feasible, it is a best practice to provide the FMLA as a benefit regardless of size. Some potential employees, who have the potential to bring significant value to your business, may not even consider working with you if you do not offer this benefit. From a diversity and inclusion standpoint, the FMLA offers those with less socio-economic means support. For more information on the FMLA, visit the US Department of Labor's website.

Crash Course Compliance Lesson #4:

Avoid Discrimination — It's Illegal!

There are many laws when it comes to discrimination and harassment that all employers are held accountable to. Those laws will be listed below in the EEOC section. However, laws aside, many companies accidentally use discriminatory practices when hiring. This is because so many states have rules and regulations with regards to hiring practices. And, asking for certain information on a job application may put you at risk for discrimination lawsuits. To protect yourself, avoid asking about the following, and speak with your attorney for a list of state laws that your organization must follow:

- <u>Convictions:</u> 35 states, and counting, prohibit employers from asking candidates about certain types of arrest or conviction records. There are caveats to this as discussed in the hiring section of the book. Know what you can and cannot ask.

- <u>Salary history:</u> In the past, it was considered a best practice to ask about one's salary history. This is now illegal in many states as lawmakers realized that this question perpetuates the gender wage gap. Know what you can and cannot ask in your particular state.

- <u>Age, birthdate or graduation year</u>: The Age Discrimination in Employment Act of 1967 protects workers who are 40 years or older and therefore you never want to ask the age, or pull any information that could indicate age, as this could be used against you later in an age discrimination lawsuit.

- <u>Citizenship:</u> To prevent national origin discrimination claims, only ask applicants if they're authorized to work in the United States, never ask if they are a citizen.

- <u>Pregnancy, children or marital status</u>: You cannot eliminate a candidate because you fear that they'll often be out of the office to care for their family. Likewise, never ask a woman or man if they plan to have kids in the coming years during a job interview. If they do not get the job, and someone who is single and plans to never have children does, you could get slapped with a lawsuit.

- <u>Religious holidays</u>: You're required to accommodate religious beliefs and practices. Candidates may think you're discriminating against them if you ask about holidays.

- <u>Alcohol, tobacco, and medical history:</u> Tobacco and alcohol usage can affect a person's quality of work, and a person's medical history can impact your company's health insurance rates. This is a fact. However, alcohol, tobacco, or medical history cannot influence your hiring decisions as it can be considered medical information. Medical information should never be a part of a hiring process and it is the employee's right to never disclose it. **Instead, ask a candidate if they've ever gotten in trouble for violating an employer's policy.** Avoid conversations about medical information entirely. What an employee or applicant wishes to disclose is up to them.

- <u>Disabilities:</u> Under the Americans with Disabilities Act, you must make reasonable accommodations for workers with disabilities. If you do not know what that includes, visit the Department of Labor website or call their helpline, and discuss with your employment lawyer about accommodation requirements.

Also, work with HR to discuss inclusive measures for assisting those with disabilities within your workforce.

- Genetic Information: Under GINA (The Genetic Information Non-Discrimination Act) employers are prohibited from using genetic information in making employment decisions, such as hiring, firing, advancement, compensation, and other terms. For example, it would be illegal for an employer to reassign an employee from a job it believes is too stressful after learning of his family's medical history of heart disease and predisposition to stroke. There are no exceptions to the prohibition on using genetic information to make employment decisions. Let us say that one more time, there are no exceptions!

Crash Course Compliance Lesson #5:

The EEOC

In the US, anti-discrimination and anti-harassment laws are enforced by an agency called the Equal Employment Opportunity Commission (EEOC). At any time, if an employee believes they have been harassed, discriminated against, or retaliated against, they can file a claim with the EEOC. The EEOC will then launch a neutral investigation into the allegations, during which the employee is protected from retaliation, and the employer is protected until a ruling is made by the EEOC.

The key as to whether or not your company is to be held to the standards of all large businesses is determined by how many employees your business has. If you have at least one employee, you are covered by the law that requires employers to provide equal pay for equal work to male and female employees.

If you have 15 to 19 employees: You are covered by the laws that prohibit discrimination based on race, color, religion, sex (including pregnancy, sexual orientation, or gender identity), national origin, disability and genetic information (including family medical history). You are also covered by the law that requires employers to provide equal pay for equal work.

If you have 20 or more employees: You are covered by the laws that prohibit discrimination based on race, color, religion, sex (including pregnancy), national origin, age (40 or older), disability and genetic information (including family medical history). You are also covered by the law that requires employers to provide equal pay for equal work.

State and/or local employment discrimination laws may also apply to your business and could be more stringent. Likewise, while you are not held to EEOC standards until you reach a specific employee number, remember that the EEOC can still decide to take up a case if one of your employees files a claim. It is up to the investigator to determine if they want to pursue it.

If you have over 20 employees, the investigator is required to pursue the investigation. Our advice is to put in place anti-discrimination and anti-harassment policies and procedures the day you hit 5 employees. All employees should receive training, and the policies need to be signed by the employees to ensure understanding. Employee handbooks should always contain these policies.

Crash Course Compliance Lesson #6:

Paid Leave — Just Do It!

Federal rules do not mandate paid time off, and many employers don't offer it which has a massive impact on employee morale. This means people must often choose between bringing home a smaller paycheck and going to work ill. To prevent this, several states have adopted paid sick laws and allow workers to use that time for themselves or a family member. Likewise, more and more states are starting to require parental leave. Speak to your employment attorney to know what is legally required, and also what is best practice in your market. Your organization will not be competitive for talent if your benefits are terrible in comparison with the other companies in your town or market.

Crash Course Compliance Lesson #7:

Retain Records — It's The Law

Retaining records can be tedious and confusing. At the Federal level, EEOC regulations require that employers keep all personnel and employment records for one year. And if an employee is terminated or resigns, those records must be kept for a year past the termination of their employment.

Under ADEA (Age Discrimination in Employment Act of 1967) employers must also keep all payroll records for three years. Additionally, employers must keep on file any employee benefit plan (such as pension and insurance plans) and any written seniority or merit system for the full period the plan or system is in effect and for at least one year after its termination.

Additionally, there are some states that have much more strict laws pertaining to record keeping with requirements to keep certain types of information for up to 7 years. Speak with your attorney to determine what laws impact your business, and then work with your HR advisor to establish a record keeping and asset management system so as to maintain compliance. For a complete list of all Federal laws impacting employers by organization size, see the next page.

COMPLIANCE CHECKLIST

Items to Review with your lawyer and HR Consultant

1+ EMPLOYEES

- Fair Labor Standards Act (FLSA)
- Immigration Reform and Control Act (IRCA)
- Employment Retirement Income Security Act (ERISA)
- Federal Income Tax Withholding
- Federal Insurance Contribution Act (FICA)
- Equal Pay Act (EPA)
- Uniform Services Employment & Reemployment Rights Act (USERRA)
- National Labor Relations Act (NLRA)
- Uniform Guidelines for Employment Selection Procedures
- Employment Polygraph Protection Act (EPPA)
- Sarbanes-Oxley Act (SOX)
- Consumer Credit Protection Act (CCPA)
- Fair and Accurate Credit Protection Act (FACT)
- Health Insurance Portability & Accountability Act (HIPAA)
- Occupational Safety and Health Act (OSHA)

15+ EMPLOYEES

- Americans with Disability Act (ADA)
- Genetic Information Nondiscrimination Act (GINA)
- Title VII, Civil Rights of 1964

20+ EMPLOYEES

- Age Discrimination in Employment Act (ADEA)
- Consolidated Omnibus Budget Reconciliation Act (COBRA)

50+ EMPLOYEES

- Affordable Care Act (ACA)
- Family & Medical Leave Act (FMLA)
- Affirmative Action Program (AAP)

VAUD CONSULTING, LLC.

14

HR Trends of the Future

The last few years have brought an avalanche of change to the HR industry. While we can't possibly cover all the trends and advancements in this book, there are three topics that we would be remiss to not include as they are topics that are bound to shape the future of the workplace.

Remote Working

With millions of Americans moving to working remotely in 2020, the work landscape has changed dramatically. What once was considered to be unorganized is now proving to be more cost effective and efficient. Recent studies done by Global Workplace Analytics have shown that businesses, on average, lose $600 billion a year to workplace distractions, and indicate that remote workers are 35% to 40% more productive than their in-office counterparts. And while we know that there are some jobs where remote work absolutely is not viable, there are many where it is. Additionally, having a choice of work environment and location is now a key factor for many job seekers when searching for a better work life balance and evaluating new career opportunities. As such, remote work is here to stay and as a small business owner, that means thinking through and creating a strong remote work policy.

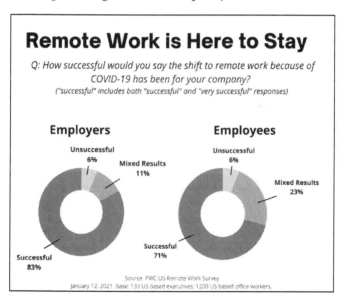

Remote Work is Here to Stay

Q: How successful would you say the shift to remote work because of COVID-19 has been for your company?
("successful" includes both "successful" and "very successful" responses)

Employers

Unsuccessful 6%
Mixed Results 11%
Successful 83%

Employees

Unsuccessful 6%
Mixed Results 23%
Successful 71%

Source: PWC US Remote Work Survey
January 12, 2021. Base: 133 US based executives; 1200 US based office workers.

While remote work is not "new," many companies have tried to avoid it as often managers grapple with questions about how to handle attendance, information security, productivity, and other concerns with employees working from different locations. That is why a remote working policy is a must.

What is in a remote work policy? A remote work policy should reflect content in your existing policies with adjustments to accommodate remote-work situations.

In general, the policies should address:

- Working schedules from a home office.
- How (and when) do employees request time off?
- What are the core hours of availability for employees working from home?
- What is the required turnaround time for responding to emails/voicemails?
- What are the expected behaviors of employees? (ie. dress code, lighting, equipment).
- How will workers compensation work?
- What are the rules with regards to storing data outside of a network server or other company managed file storage program like Dropbox or SharePoint?

Other Standard Operating Procedures (SOPs) to consider might include:

- How often do remote employees check in with their managers?

- What digital chat channels, text, email systems etc. will the organization use in order to drive collaboration with co-workers who are not in office?

- Do employees need their cameras on during virtual meetings? (And should they use a virtual background?)

- What communications systems and project management systems etc. will be used to track work and progress?

The list goes on…

Without defined parameters and policies, expectations are unclear, and a few employees will always try to take advantage. In order to hold employees accountable, employees need to be made aware of all guidelines. One-size-fits-all may not be the answer, either, and if some roles have different expectations than others, or are highly crucial to organizational success, customizing your job descriptions should outline the remote version of the position.

Additionally, every employer needs to determine what will be provided in terms of equipment so employees can do their jobs. In the case of standard office equipment, employers have the choice of issuing laptops or desktops and cell phones or asking employees to use their own, known as a Bring Your Own Device (BYOD) policy. Asking employees to use their own devices can be tricky if you fail to check state and local regulations. In some states, personal equipment used for business must be reimbursed to employees as they are considered supplies. Make sure to reach out to your employment lawyer before creating any BYOD policy. As a personal recommendation, we encourage avoiding such policies as it also can cause very messy exits and even employers getting dragged into the personal lives of their employees due to things like divorce subpoenas.

Another factor to consider when it comes to remote working is security. If remote working becomes a norm, the creation of an IT plan, with a dedicated IT point of contact, will absolutely be necessary. Sadly, small companies without traditional IT support are left vulnerable to hacking as employees begin working on unsecured home networks, from coffee shops, etc. VPN software might be needed and employees will need to be trained on security concerns and how to properly use company equipment.

Bottom line, remote working is here to stay but it requires strong policies and IT infrastructure and support in order to protect your organization.

Diversity and Inclusion: A Strategic Imperative

Diversity & Inclusion
The Future Workforce

2019 In 2019, most new hires of prime age workers (ages 25-54) were people of color for the first time, according to a Washington Post Analysis

2020 In 2020, the US population under the age of 18 became a "majority-minority," where the number of individuals who are multiracial and racial and ethnic minorities exceeded those of whites. By 2044, the full population will reach that status

In 2020, an increasing number of individuals-- 4.5% -- identify as LGBTQIA with those in younger generations more likely to self-identify (56% of LGBTQIA adults are under age 35)

2028 The Latinx population is expected to make up more than 20% of the labor force by 2028, up from 17.5% in 2018.

2048 The number of individuals who are multiracial and ethnic minorities is projected to exceed those of whites.

2060 The census projects that whites will comprise 36% of the US population under the age of 18.

for more details, visit
www.brookings.edu

The rise of diversity and inclusion initiatives and organizational focus over the last several years marks an important shift in what diversity, equity and inclusion (DEI) means in the workplace. By the year 2048, the number of individuals who are multiracial and/or minorities will exceed the number of whites (see the infographic above). As it should be, gone are the days when diversity and inclusion efforts are simply to check a box. The backgrounds of the leaders and teams within your organization should and do require a broad and diverse range of skill sets. In order to tackle diversity issues, industries must act to evolve their sector into one that attracts, retains and reflects all members of society.

As a small business owner diversity, equity and inclusion should become a focus within your organization, not just because it is the right thing to do, but also because your business will not survive if inclusion is not top of mind. How you treat your employees matters. Your organization's values matter. If you are struggling to attract and retain diverse talent, find a diversity and inclusion practitioner who can assist you in creating a culture of belonging. Be sure that culture, and your values, are reflected within all aspects of your company— your handbook, website, and policies and procedures. Your ability to innovate and remain competitive depends on it. But oftentimes, small businesses and start-ups fail to take DEI on as a business imperative.

Becoming more inclusive is not just a matter of adding new protected categories and identities to anti-discrimination laws. Rather, DEI in the workplace now has completely flipped in how diversity is considered. Gone are the days where diversity is viewed defensively — or as legal or ethical compliances. The broader vision and goal of a successful diversity and inclusion initiative can be summed up as a focus on diversity of thought. This is the business case for a successful DEI initiative within a small business. Diversity of thought covers the unique perspectives that all individuals bring to the table. The expanding range of perspectives and cultural experiences bring about greater innovation and problem-solving. Truly inclusive organizations will also see an increase in recruitment and retention and in their brand/image.

But without a huge HR budget, how do small businesses approach DEI? Effective inclusive practices are not implemented without a conscious effort. It takes strong leadership to guide the process and a staff willing to establish a structured, but flexible, framework in which inclusive practices may be seamlessly integrated. In order to assist with this process, at a minimum we encourage the following:

Establish a DEI vision statement.

A diversity and inclusion vision statement demonstrates a company's commitment to building an inclusive, varied workplace welcoming to people of all backgrounds. Much like a mission and values statement, the diversity and inclusion statement is, ideally, more than just a marketing exercise. It should guide your hiring, employee benefits, customer service and workplace culture. In addition, the creation of a DEI vision statement helps inform recommended policy and procedure changes.

Establishing a DEI vision statement is best achieved through an inclusive diversity visioning process. An inclusive diversity visioning process solicits input from all employees and leadership. Through this process, all staff are prompted to discuss and define the type of organizational culture they envision. By soliciting and incorporating employee feedback, organizations yield maximum employee buy-in for the guiding DEI vision.

Establish a DEI Council

A diversity, equity and inclusion council is a task force of diverse team members who are responsible for helping bring about the cultural, and possibly ethical, changes necessary for your business.

This can include, but is not limited to, data collection, training recommendations and development, focus groups and policy recommendations. Leadership should always help craft the DEI Council's strategic goals, as well as to support any existing or future initiatives, such as supplier diversity programs, marketing, and/or recruitment processes. This council should also have an executive sponsor or someone from the senior leadership team as a member.

Hire an outside DEI consulting firm to audit your organization's policies.

A key component to any successful diversity and inclusion initiative is understanding the equity and inclusiveness of your organization's policies and procedures. With a full DEI Audit, you will be able to identify ways to make your policies more inclusive, competitive, and meaningful to your employees. Unlike a compliance-based audit, DEI policy audits review and identify structural barriers to inclusion within your organization's HR policies and the extent to which inclusion exists from an administrative and Human Resources perspective.

Offer DEI training to all staff.

Often given a bad reputation, training your workforce on the benefits of diversity, equity, and inclusion, as well as working to develop their interpersonal skills, will go a long way in fostering a culture of DEI. It also is imperative that employees understand your organization's DEI vision statement, and the behaviors that are expected of them moving forward. Good DEI training goes well beyond conversations around anti-harassment and anti-discrimination and covers topics such as navigating difficult dialogues, race equity, microaggressions, unconscious bias, and managerial skills. While no single organization will require the same types of training, the DEI council should work with leadership each year to establish what training would provide the greatest impact to improving belonging.

Social Media — it's complicated

The last trend/topic we would be remiss if we did not bring up is social media. Social media is a double-edged sword for employers. On one hand it serves as a free promotional tool for your company, and with the right social media team can help take your organization to the next level. On the other hand, it has introduced the need to regulate employee communications because each one of your employees on social media is promoting their opinions, feelings, and personal lives. The lines between "personal" and "professional" are increasingly blurred online. As a result, all companies would do well to establish workplace social media policies to ensure that no trade secrets, brand negativity, or unethical behavior is occurring online. Such a policy gives employees a clear understanding of what they are allowed to post on their own channels and what is off-limits.

Guidelines to consider for a general social media policy should include rules around proprietary information, opinions that are not reflective of the organization's values, bullying, and relationships.

All employees are ambassadors of your brand. If they are about to post something that they would be ashamed to say out loud, or that can haunt them in the future, then they should think twice about posting it.

As an employer, you can mitigate this risk by educating employees and protecting your brand at the same time. In an era of oversharing in which everything seems to be fair game, your company will avoid damaging its reputation by having these policies in place.

15

NAVIGATING THE FUTURE

Congratulations! You've made it through to the end. HR policy, rules, regulations and processes are not the most exciting stuff to learn about when it comes to business. Of course, you would much rather focus your time on what you love to do, that's why you took the risk and leapt into the business world.

Unfortunately, as you learned as a child, you can't always do what you like to do. Life is full of those nagging little things that have to be done to make things right. And that, in a nutshell, is HR. It's not fun but it can sink your business like a U-boat sinking ships in World War II — quick, unseen and in a ball of flames.

As a small business owner, having a strong approach to HR is the only clear way to achieving business stability and growth. And, as we have thoroughly discussed, HR is not for the thin skinned.

When a company hits about 15-25 employees, it may be time to start thinking about having a dedicated HR professional on staff. This number may vary depending on the type of business, growth and how much time managers are spending on HR functions. When a company is experiencing rapid growth or a high rate of employee problems, it may be best to bring on a full time HR person even sooner. For startups or businesses with young founders, sooner is better.

Until you reach the point where you have a full time HR professional, there are a couple options for covering this part of running a business. The easiest approach is to assign HR duties to your manager of operations, or whoever manages the day-to-day operations of the business. It is important that this person attend regular HR seminars and get an HR certification which can be self-studied. Local seminars are a great way to network with people in HR—people who could be a good resource later on when you have an HR question or need to hire a consultant.

HR consultants can also provide support to small businesses. Many offer on-call services to answer HR questions, compliance checks, templates for OTS use, employee handbook reviews, DEI, and HR training. Regardless of what approach you take to cover your HR needs, including HR as part of your business strategy is key to your organizational success.

At the end of the day the people part of your business should be fun. The policy part of the people side, not so much. HR requires communication, organization and record keeping. It requires you to listen and learn and accept the reality of the needs of your people along with the needs of your business.

The future of HR, just like the future of business, will continue to evolve and change. It is safe to assume that more protections will be put in place to ensure that people, from all walks of life, are treated fairly in their employment. Technology has impacted every aspect of business. HR is no different. If anything it has quickened the pace of change and the expectation that change is understood and quickly assimilated into your business.

There is an old saying, "…ignorance is no excuse…" This is particularly true in HR. Not only is it not an excuse, it is not a defense. You can save yourself a lot of time, energy and money by making sure that your team is aware of the applicable HR principles, policies and laws that apply to your business regardless of your industry sector or size. Failure to do that can steal your dreams.

HR Case Study

Sylvia Jordan was a successful entrepreneur. Her small business had, over the last 4-5 years, grown through her and her small team's hard work. She was living her dreams. Her business, *Joyce Toppings*, designs, makes and sells 100% natural fabric blouses and shirts.

For years Sylvia and her small team were able to make all of the blouses and shirts, but then that got to be too much. The money was coming in so Sylvia outsourced some products. Sales continued to increase, but Sylvia noticed that quality and customer satisfaction ratings were slipping. Orders were being delivered later than promised. Orders were shipped to the wrong address. Orders weren't entirely shipped.

This worried Sylvia immensely. The business that she had built her life upon, which was named after her late Aunt Joyce who had significant business struggles when Sylvia was growing up, was in trouble. She knew it just like she knew when one of her kids wasn't being totally honest. She could feel it in her bones. And then an unexpected email showed up.

Most of Sylvia's products were sold online though the *Joyce Toppings* website. The brand had very little retail exposure, in either the physical or digital store fronts. Sylvia was proud of what she and her team had built, and she knew that one day, after these problems were fixed, they could do a lot more.

But the email...

Hi Sylvia,

We're a large global provider of boutique high end products that are environmentally friendly. We have partnered with numerous boutique shops over our 20-year history. Each year our select editions sell out.

We would like to feature a unique Joyce Toppings collection, which would be an entire women's and men's line. As this would be a primary product for this season the volumes would be very high for a condensed period of time. We will require the first products in 120 days.

As an add on, our sister organization, a large national retailer, would like a Joyce Toppings designed brand that is sold in each of its retail locations. They are looking at long-term (3+ year agreement for high volume seasonal designs). For planning purposes, this would begin in 180 days for the first shipments.

We look forward to discussing the details of this relationship in the next few days.

Best,
Alicia Ferguson

Reflection:

The decision to outsource is a complicated one. Cost savings is part of the equation, but if that's not the main reason to do it, it could be a bad idea, and undermine a company's potential for long term success. Unlike managing employees and processes in house, when a company outsources, they are putting much of the responsibility under someone else's control.

What mistake did Sylvia realize she had made in outsourcing, and what HR and business implications did that decision have?

The email was short and to the point. A major retailer, who Slyvia always wanted to work with, wanted to roll out a line designed by *Joyce Toppings* specifically for its high-end customers. They were offering top dollar.

Sylvia needed a team that she could depend on to make this work. That meant that most of the previously outsourced manufacturing and fulfillment would have to come back in house. That would start to fix the problems and the damage done to the brand, but 90 days is not much time.

Then, she had to gear up not one but TWO product ramp ups from design, through production, with high volume distribution. She had 45 days to get going and about 90 days before orders would start being processed in order to meet the seasonal demand.

90 days…Ninety days…Three months…

Sylvia needed to identify, interview, hire, onboard and train team members for manufacturing, customer service and shipping—at a minimum—to meet the needs of the seasonal demands.

Here's what happened: Sylvia knew that she needed help. She remembered a workshop session that she attended about quickly increasing your small business workforce to fulfill a big contract. It was focused on companies bidding on Request for Proposals (RFPs) and while at the time it was not something she was planning to do, something told her to go and learn more.

Sylvia had always been one to follow her instincts and that was probably what made her company so successful, or at least, so she thought. Her company was comfortable but not a huge success. It had so much more potential. There was a lot of demand for all-natural fabric tops. She had an opportunity to take her business to a whole new level, one that she had merely dreamt about before she opened Alicia's email.

Now it was real!

The business needed a process. She remembered the workshop trainer emphasizing the importance of taking the time to develop a standard process to go through fast hiring. Each position should have a job description that highlights the specific requirements, expectations and skill sets that each position requires.

Oh my gosh, Sylvia thought. *I need job descriptions; I need to know what positions we need to fill. I need to develop the operations plan so that we know which positions we need and which ones we need to fill right away. And I need that immediately so that we can start to find those people.*

These thoughts raced through her mind as she mindlessly drove to the other side of town to pick up her kids from their music classes. They had moved closer to her office a few months ago but she, nor her children, were quite ready to let go of their tried-and-true activities and friends. Let them get a little more adjusted in their new schools and then they would see.

And then her thoughts came back to…90 Days…

Reflections

HR is a complicated and diverse field. How should Sylvia approach her need to scale while also avoiding the pitfall of filling HR with an inexperienced player?

Is Sylvia even ready to hire for an HR role or should she outsource?

What advice would an employment lawyer provide Sylvia with at this time?

The next morning Sylvia got her small team together. It was a small team. First, there was Janice, the office manager, who originally joined Sylvia to answer the phone and handle all of the orders after Sylvia ran a short late-night tv commercial.

Then there was Allan. He was an odd duck, and an amazing customer service coordinator. He had a way of making the customer feel happy that they called in to complain because they got to talk to him. He just had a special magic. After customers worked with Allan, they were happy, no matter how upset they were when they first dialed in. He was gold.

There were also the 7 ladies who were working in production. They made the products that Sylvia designed. And then there was Candy. Candy ran shipping, and she ran it like a clock. Shipping problems were so rare that they were almost unheard of when Candy ran all of the shipping. Candy's flawless shipping had been outsourced because at the time, it was less expensive than increasing internal capacity. Problems didn't arise until Sylvia outsourced the shipping and Candy had no control over how things were done. In fact, Allan wasn't hired until after the third-party manufacturers and shippers started fouling things up.

Sylvia sat them down and told them about the problems and about the email. She told them about how she saw this as an opportunity to learn a lesson and grow in many ways at the same time. She told them that it would be very, very hard, but not impossible. She told them that they would all have to work together in a way to build a foundation for lots of new people to join them without destroying the magic that they all had working together.

They were not surprised. They all knew that the brand was good. They all knew that they could do it better than anyone and they all loved the fact that things would be brought back inside and provide them and others with job opportunities. That was exciting. They also knew that there was a lot of risk because it all had to happen fast, too fast in Allan's estimation. Not fast enough in Candy's. That was good Sylvia thought, there is balance on the team...at least in thought.

The group talked for over an hour and then Sylvia asked them to think about one thing for the next few days. That one thing was captured in the question, "What type of person would be the best to help make the team better?" This wasn't a role or skill-based question, it was a character and culture question and it is the first question that one could ask the team before a major hiring spree.

Everyone thought about the question. Sylvia emphasized that they should not answer right away, but that they should give it serious thought and would come back together in two days to discuss it.

Reflections

What type of person would help make your team better?

The answer to this question is important. It is much more important than many new leaders think. In too many cases people hire for skill sets only in a crunch and end up with a few people who are not good fits. In some cases, they end up with people who actually distract from the mission and drag the team down, negatively impacting morale and productivity. Asking this question early, and using the answers as a guiding star, is worth every minute that your business spends on it. Unfortunately, Sylvia did not have much time to spend with her team and consider this question. That's why when they came back together a few days later she dove right in...

"You guys are the backbone of this business. You know how to get things done in a way that makes the customer happy and makes us money. You guys work together in ways that always amaze me, finding a way to get it done. And the crazy thing is that all of you are so different, but yet you work together so well. Why is that?"

"Because we believe in the products and what we are doing!" said one of the grandmotherly types, Rose, who worked in production. Rose had been the 4th person to join the business. She continued, "we know what we offer to the customers. We see ourselves as the customers and because we can identify with them, we want to make them happy."

Allan added, "Our products are primo and our customers know that, but they are also affordable. Even though many of our products are getting pricier, we have never forgotten the people that we started making the blouses and shirts for. They are affordable, high quality all-natural products and that is important to me."

After about 45 minutes it was clear that the team was in agreement on why they worked together so well, and the type of person that could fit in and add value to make the team better. They also agreed that it is better to hire a person that is a good character fit with lower skills and help them improve their skills, than it is to hire someone with top notch skills who might be harder to work with. There was unanimous agreement from the team on that. Sylvia smiled on the inside like she hadn't in years.

Reflections:

You know that if you're leading a rapidly growing company, you need expertise that includes administrative, tactical, and strategic abilities from your HR team. It's tricky to find all of those skills in one person. Syvlia recognizes this, and also knows that she needs her team's buy-in and support to even attempt to meet Alicia's request. Sylvia's approach is strong.

What other HR and strategy conversations should Sylvia be having with her team?

The key qualities that the team felt made them work so well together were:

1. Belief in the products and the value that they delivered to customers.
2. Respect for each other and their lives.
3. Willingness to help each other out and hold each other accountable.

These were fantastic. So, these were the key qualities that Sylvia had to find a way to identify in new hires. But then it hit her, she wasn't going to be the one working side-by-side with most of these new hires—the team was—and they were clear on what they wanted in new teammates. So, Sylvia put together a hiring committee to make sure that the person fit the basic values and culture of *Joyce Toppings*. They would do the first round of interviews for each position.

But she still needed help. And now she needed to make sure that the interview committee did everything the right way. Sylvia had to find someone with significant HR experience to help her get through this fast-paced hiring and ramp up sprint that she was beginning. So, she called her friend Pam, who was an HR manager at a medium sized company in town. She and Pam had met years ago and were casual friends who got together with other friends every few months for drinks and to catch up.

Sylvia asked Pam if she knew any tried and true HR generalists who work with small businesses to help them set up a fast hiring support system. She needed someone who could help with identifying the right candidates, recruiting and vetting them, onboarding them and training them to fit the needs of the team. Sylvia saw this as a one-year project. She also knew that she would probably hire the person after 6-9 months to build on what was already in place, but she felt it was too early to mention that. She felt that would come together on its own if it was right.

Pam knew a few people who Sylvia might want to talk to. They all had experience with small businesses in widely different industries. Pam mentioned that some were more traditional types while others were geared more towards helping companies set up remote policies and systems for their people. Sylvia knew that she wanted a mix of both, due to the nature of what they did, but she was open to talk to those from both spectrums to see who was a better fit based on approach, fit, schedule and likability. Sylvia was going to apply the cultural guiding principles that the team set to the selection of the HR advisor.

Sylvia met with 3 HR professionals over many days to get a feel for their abilities, their passion for what she and her team were doing, and fit with the *Joyce Toppings* team. She selected Denise for the role. Denise was smart, accomplished, professional and very well respected in the HR advisory industry. Business owners that she worked with raved about her. She was warm, easy to talk to and took a liking to several of the *Joyce Toppings* team members right away. She had an authenticity that was apparent, compassionate and firm. Denise immediately understood Sylvia's challenges, her vision, and her immediate needs, and she laid out an initial plan for each month to move towards the 90-day (now 82-day) goal of getting ready for major growth.

Denise came in the following week with a list of key points that she had discussed with the interview committee. These key points were basically a primer of things that you can and can't ask in an interview. She and Sylvia agreed that though Denise had talked to everyone that they should set up a documented training session to make sure that everyone was clear in their understanding of what they could and could not do in the interview process.

The team training went smoothly. Sylvia had an outline of the initial new hires that she was going to need. She modified her old biz plan with a focus on the operations section to really dig deep into the company's needs over the next 6-9 months. This was just the first phase, and she knew it, but it was also the most important. She thought back to something her grandfather used to say, "How you start is how you finish." Start strong, stay focused, finish strong and enjoy the results were her game plan.

Sylvia looked at the key positions that needed to be filled immediately to maintain the standards that she felt were acceptable. There were 3 roles that needed to be filled to meet the deadlines. All 3 roles had several openings. Training could be combined for some and overlapped for others. Sylvia knew that what seemed impossible just a week or two ago was now coming into focus. She had to focus on what the team was accomplishing and where it was headed, not the heaping mound of work that it had to do to get there.

Sylvia wrote basic job descriptions for each of the roles, and then sent them to the people on the team to edit. Then, she sent them to the people that would have to coordinate, interact with, or share information with the people in that new role.

Once this was complete, she sent the job descriptions to Denise for a clean-up and to put them in a proper format to fit into the growing HR system. By the end of the week, all of the job descriptions were done, and Denise started working on the recruitment ads. Her goal was to get them to Sylvia late Friday evening for approval so that they could start running over the weekend.

By Tuesday of the following week the digital ads that *Joyce Toppings* had placed were getting inundated with applications. "Wow," Sylvia thought, that was a great sign. Denise recommended that she screen all of the applications first to make sure that they are complete. Those that were not complete would be filtered out. The applications that made it past the initial screening would be sent to the interview committee to see which ones they wanted to bring in. For each position Denise had them narrow down to the top 5 candidates. This was done in two days, which was a grueling process. The team was tired, their eyes hurt from reading the applications, but they were all excited to start scheduling interviews so that they could start building the team—and the future. The team's commitment to push through this tough process was a testament to the desire that everyone had for the business to thrive.

Denise started scheduling interviews for early the following week with most of them scheduled for Wednesday. The interview team knew the interview questions to ask, and Denise was there to guide the process as it went off track from time to time. She was also there to pick up signals that may not align with what the interviewee was saying. Throughout the interview process Denise identified two candidates that misrepresented some aspect of themselves. She was sure that the oversights were minor, but the team disqualified the candidates because they felt they were being dishonest and disrespected. It violated one of their values—mutual respect. These guiding principles that Sylvia and the team took a little time to think about really were setting the tone for the day to day functioning of the business.

Within the first month Sylvia had hired 9 of the 15 people that they would need to meet the minimum growth needs. Denise had spent two weeks interviewing the key team members and the people that performed the jobs to put together a training program for each role. It was ready just when the first new hires were ready to start.

To help ensure that first week with the new hires would go smoothly, Denise put together an onboarding package. It gave the company history, the person's role, where they fit in the organization, key company rules and protocols, benefits and insurance forms and some company swag. Denise also made sure that every new hire had a sponsor that they could connect with to help them fit into the company quicker. The sponsor introduced them to people, stressed the company values and generally tried to be a good guide and work friend to help ease them into the company and its culture.

Wow…as Sylvia sat back over a glass of wine at dinner to thank Pam for guiding her to Denise, she had to marvel at the progress that they had made in the first 35 or so days. They still had a little less than 60 days to go, and they were already starting to train the first group of hires. She knew that she still needed 6 more people, at a minimum. She would really feel comfortable with 10-12 more people, but the company could get by with 6, for now.

Reflections

- What compliance issues should Denise and Sylvia be taking note of as the team expands?

- What HR best practices should Sylvia seek Denise's advice on?

- In the real world, it is not always possible to pull the whole team together to assist with onboarding and hiring. Going forward, what standardized practices should Sylvia work with Denise to develop so that hiring becomes streamlined and does not disrupt the business?

- Had Sylvia not hired HR help and attempted to take on this process herself, what possible issues might she have faced?

Sylvia decided, after talking to Pam, that she would bring the team together to do a performance analysis to not only acknowledge and celebrate all of the things that they did right, but to share ideas on what they could do better. Finding the additional people that they need may be harder but if their process and appeal was improved it may even things out. Sylvia, not for one second, was going to take her foot off the gas because although the people part of the growth plan was key, it was only one part of the growth plan.

When Sylvia got in her car, she called Denise. If they couldn't find the full-time people that they needed in the near future, could they find part time team members? There were plenty of college kids who were looking for meaningful work. She had even met some at a business association meeting. They were smart, eager, talented and wanted to do something to help make the world a better place. Many of the college students that she met over the last few years sought jobs or careers that reflected their values rather than just provided them with a paycheck. How could they use this to help take *Joyce Toppings* into the future?

Denise called a few of the informal team leaders and asked them to discuss the part time team member concept. All of the team members, every single one of them, thought that it was great. Even better, most of them knew people that they thought would be a good fit for part time work. It didn't take more than a few days for the team to have identified a list of over 70 great part time candidates for production, shipping and customer service. It was good that they had options to hire the people that they needed in phases. Still, Sylvia was nervous about having a high percentage of her team, possibly as many as 25 people, work on a part time basis.

Interviewing so many people for all the positions was going to be a real burden for the team. It was going to take some time because all of these new faces would take time to integrate. Sylvia wanted to make sure that the phase in plan was slow enough to give new people a few weeks to acclimate before another wave was phased in. She wanted to avoid the drip, drip, drip of daily hiring and decided to foster a sort of cohort attitude for each new group of team members. This would take some planning, and would be a little more time consuming to set up and operate, but given her time constraints, this seemed the most structured and controlled way to approach growth.

Reflections

- What benefits, and legal compliance requirements, will need to be taken into consideration for hiring 25 part time workers?
- What communication tools, time management tools, and feedback mechanisms will managers need to deploy to ensure efficiency?
- With well over 70 employees, what additional leadership roles should Denise and Sylvia be looking to fill?
- How might Denise and Sylvia tackle HR trends like diversity and inclusion, social media, and remote working?
- What policies and/or documents should be created beyond compliance related requirements?

15 Months Later...

The team has risen to the occasion. *Joyce Toppings* has over 70 employees, 40 of whom are part time. The company's sales has increased over 350% over the last year and it is on pace to grow at an even faster pace over the next 15-18 months. Sylvia is excited that her company, the company that she created, the company that she pushed and pulled and cajoled and financed in life altering ways, was growing to the point that investment bankers and private equity managers were starting to call her pitching their capital raising and investment partnership track records. It was heady stuff... a little too heady.

But none of it would have been possible without the team that came together 15 months ago. They put together the pieces to find, hire, onboard, train, and integrate the new team members — both part-time and full-time — into the company, the culture, the products and the operation. It was not without glitches, but all things considered, the process was fairly smooth. Once the kinks were worked out, the cohort idea that Sylvia envisioned had been a great team building and camaraderie exercise. It helped everyone communicate and laugh and have a common business cultural reference point.

Glossary

ACA—Affordable Care Act

The Affordable Care Act (ACA), commonly known as Obamacare, is a United States federal government act that was signed into law by President Obama on March 23, 2010. For more information on how this law impacts your business, please contact your benefits advisor or an employment lawyer.

ADEA—Age Discrimination in Employment Act of 1967

The Age Discrimination in Employment Act of 1967 (ADEA) protects certain applicants and employees 40 years of age and older from discrimination on the basis of age in hiring, promotion, discharge, compensation, or terms, conditions or privileges of employment.

DEI —Diversity, Equity, and Inclusion

EEOC—Equal Employment Opportunity Commission

The U.S. Equal Employment Opportunity Commission is a large federal agency that was established via the 1964 Civil Rights Act to administer and enforce civil rights laws against workplace discrimination. For more information, visit https://www.eeoc.gov/

FLSA—Fair Labor Standards Act

The Fair Labor Standards Act of 1938 is a United States labor law that creates the right to a minimum wage, and "time-and-a-half" overtime pay when people work over forty hours a week. It also prohibits employment of minors in "oppressive child labor". Updates to this law are ever expanding and should be monitored closely.

FMLA—Family Medical Leave Act

The Family and Medical Leave Act of 1993 is a United States labor law requiring covered employers to provide employees with job-protected and unpaid leave for qualified medical and family reasons. Many companies have expanded policies with some states offering additional benefits.

FTE—Full-Time Employee or Full-Time Equivalent

A FTE is any employee who normally works 30 hours or more per week and is eligible for company benefits.

GINA—Genetic Information Non-Discrimination Act

The Genetic Information Nondiscrimination Act of 2008, is an Act of Congress in the United States designed to prohibit some types of genetic discrimination. Genetic information, therefore, must be protected within the workplace. Many states have more stringent laws than the federal government when it comes to genetic information. For additional information, contact your employment lawyer or a employment lawyer within the state of question.

HR—Human Resources

Human Resources is the set of the people who make up the workforce of an organization, business sector, industry, or economy. A narrower concept is human capital.

OTS—Off-the-Shelf

Commercial off-the-shelf or commercially available off-the-shelf products are packaged solutions which are then adapted to satisfy the needs of the purchasing organization, rather than the commissioning of custom-made solutions.

PTE—Part-Time Employee or Part-Time Equivalent
PTE refers to any employee who works under 30 hours a week and who is not eligible for benefits. PTE employees differ from 1099s as they are not responsible for their own taxes, but they do have to follow the same policies and procedures as employees.

RFP—Request for Proposal
A request for proposal is a document that solicits proposals, often made through a bidding process, by an agency or company interested in procurement of a commodity or service to potential suppliers.

SHRM—Society of Human Resource Management
The Society for Human Resource Management is a professional Human Resources membership association headquartered in Alexandria, Virginia. SHRM promotes the role of HR as a profession and provides education, certification, and networking to its members, while lobbying Congress on issues pertinent to labor management. To learn more visit https://www.shrm.org/

ADDITIONAL RESOURCES:

Department of Labor
https://www.dol.gov/

National Association of Employment Lawyers
https://www.nela.org/

ABOUT THE AUTHORS

Art Espey has been involved with numerous businesses both domestically and internationally over the last 30+ years. Through his experiences in growing a business to the top 100 of its industry and as a leader in an Inc. 500 company, Art has developed productivity and communication strategies that help small businesses and startups be more effective and more efficient – turning your revenue into profit faster.

Laura Bowser is the Founder of Vaud Consulting—a DEI and HR operations management consulting firm working to advance more culturally inclusive and equitable workforces. Prior to launching Vaud Consulting, Laura was the CEO of an award-winning diversity, equity and inclusion firm. During her tenure as CEO, the company was recognized as a Best for the World diversity, equity and inclusion (DEI) solutions provider by B Lab as featured in the NYT. Laura is also Chair of the Virginia's Alzheimer's and Related Disorders Commission, Vice Chair of Data Friendly Spaces, board member at Read to Them, and previous founding member of the Burke-Paine Society.

Made in the USA
Middletown, DE
16 October 2021